The Miracle of Bryan Pearce

To Jain Wallis
love from
Bryan

C. J. Stevens

John Wade, Publisher

Published by John Wade, Publisher
P.O. Box 303
Phillips, Maine 04966

The Miracle of Bryan Pearce
1. Bryan Pearce and his mother Mary Pearce—Biography
2. 20th and 21st Century—Bryan Pearce, Retarded English Painter
3. Great Britain—20th Century Art Scene, St. Ives, Cornwall

Library of Congress Control Number: 2003116278

ISBN 1-882425-20-0 cloth
ISBN 1-882425-21-9 paperback

Manufactured in the United States of America

FIRST EDITION

ACKNOWLEDGMENTS

I am grateful to Mary Pearce for her friendship and generosity in sharing memories, family photographs, and illustrations of her son's work. Her courage is this book's inspiration.

I owe a debt of gratitude to Ellery Borow, Bryan Lumbra, Denis Mitchell, Kate Nicholson, Misomé Peile, Vera Rayhart, Ivor Short, and Barbara Tribe.

Denys Val Baker's *Britain's Art Colony by the Sea*, published by Sansom & Company, 2000, and first issued in 1959 by George Ronald, was particularly helpful in profiling the St. Ives art scene.

I am indebted to the authors and publishers of the following books for permission to quote material:
The Primitive Art of Bryan Pearce by George T. Noszlopy, Taurus Artists, 1964
The Path of the Son by Ruth Jones, Sheviock Gallery Publications, 1976 and 1993
Bryan Pearce - A Private View by Marion Whybrow, St. Ives Printing & Publishing, 1985
Chronicles of Courage - Very Special Artists, Jean Kennedy Smith and George Plimpton, Random House, 1993
The Innocent Eye: Primitive and Naïve Painters in Cornwall by Marion Whybrow, Sansom & Company, 1999
Bryan Pearce: The Artist and his Work by Janet Axten, Sansom & Company, 2000.

I thank these copyright holders for providing catalog introductions:
Peter Lanyon © the estate of the author 1964 for St. Martin's Gallery
Alan Bowness © the author 1966 for New Art Centre
H. S. Ede © the estate of the author 1982 for Falmouth Art Gallery.

Additional acknowledgments are made to the following copyright holders:
William Leah © the author 1985 for his letter to the *St. Ives Parish Magazine*
William Cooper © the author 2000 for "Bryan Pearce - A Reminiscence" appearing in *Bryan Pearce: The Artist and his Work* by Janet Axten.

I thank the following publications for granting me permission to quote from their files: *Cornish Magazine, The Cornishman, The Cornish Review, Daily Word, Freedom, The Guardian, St. Ives Times & Echo,* and *Western Morning News.*

Janet Axten was of invaluable help in the final stages of this book.

I am grateful to Mary Adams, Cecil Collins, Keith Colquhoun, Michael Holloway, Ruth Jones, Dr. Brian Kirman, Sheila Lanyon, Ian Mayes, Arthur Moyse, Wendy Oliver, Donald Rawe, Frank Ruhrmund, Charles Thomas, Michael Tresillian, and Dr. Christopher Woodard.

Selections from interviews with Mary Pearce were first published in volume XXVII, Number 4, Autumn 1973 of the *Western Humanities Review* and later reprinted in *Bryan Pearce: The Artist and his Work* by Janet Axten, Sansom & Company, 2000.

For granting me permission to reprint photographic illustrations, I thank Janet Axten; the Museum of Modern Art, Oxford; Mary Pearce; Marion Whybrow; and the several owners of paintings in private collections.

Most of all, I am indebted to my wife, Stella Stevens. Her encouragement and guidance made this book possible.

NOTE
Readers will find variations in some abbreviations and the spelling of certain words. (e.g. St. Ives-St Ives and harbor-harbour) This is because all quoted material has been rendered in its original state.

PREFACE

It was through my mother-in-law, Vera Rayhart, that I first learned of Mary and Walter Pearce and their retarded son, Bryan, who was beginning to achieve widespread recognition as a painter. This was during the winter of 1967-1968 when my wife, Stella, and I rented a cottage in St. Ives, Cornwall, England. Mrs. Rayhart, who was staying nearby at the Porthminster Hotel, became acquainted with Misomé Peile, a local artist, and it was Misomé who introduced Vera to this St. Ives family. "You must see the paintings," I was urged, "and hear Mary's story."

The Pearces' son, Bryan, was born in 1929, an apparently healthy baby. He had, however, phenylketonuria, a metabolic disease caused by a defective gene from each parent. Without treatment this condition, in which the protein from certain foods cannot be broken down, inevitably leads to impaired brain development. Bryan's disorder remained undiagnosed until he was an adult. After they were assured by doctors that it was "safe" to have another child, their daughter, Margaretta, was born in 1941. The new arrival appeared normal, but soon there were signs of retardation.

Walter and Mary were told that Bryan would never reach an average level of competence, and one specialist informed the couple that their son might get on sufficiently in life "to be able to do a simple mending job on a pair of shoes." Margaretta's impairments were more noticeable in early childhood: she couldn't talk, walk, had to be spoonfed, and there were frequent convulsions.

The Pearces braved the devastating reality of their predicament and vowed to do everything they could for their children. Walter's butcher shop allowed him some escape from the daily heartbreak of watching over Bryan and Margaretta, but for Mary there was no release—her life seemed to be a series of complications squeezed in a setting that offered few assurances. One poignancy that captivated all who were acquainted with her undertaking was the burst of fresh courage after each setback— she refused to relinquish hope.

Margaretta did learn to walk and eventually she achieved muscular coordination, though she never was able to talk. Joyous in her responses to the world, the girl, at times, appeared to be at the threshold of some normalcy, but when the anticipated breakthrough seemed near there were reversals. Grand mal incidents often occurred during the early morning hours, and for more than ten years Mary listened in her half sleep for ominous sounds in the next room. One night she didn't hear her daughter. Margaretta had suffocated while having an attack—she was nineteen years old.

Bryan was sent to a school for the retarded in London, and he was under custodial care from the age of ten to sixteen. Upon his return to St. Ives, Walter and Mary were faced with the problem of finding some sort of employment for their frustrated and often angry teenager. A temporary solution was having him scrub pots and pans at the butcher shop, and in time Bryan learned how to twist sausages and to mince meat.

One day Mary brought home a child's coloring book and coaxed her twenty-four-year-old son to fill in a page of bold outlines with watercolors. He did the task beautifully, became interested, and this was the beginning of one of the most astonishing adventures in twentieth century painting.

I recall clearly our first visit with the Pearces at their home overlooking Porthmeor Beach. Mary greeted Stella and me at the door, introduced herself, and led us into the lounge to meet her husband and Bryan. Walter Pearce was himself—just the kind of person I had imagined: warm and courteous with a hint of shyness in the presence of strangers. Mary was more outgoing; she was easy to be with and delightfully informal. The surprise of the evening was Bryan. He rose from his chair, shook hands with a firm grip, and listened closely as we chatted. Two or three times, he contributed a few words which were politely delivered and germane. He looked so intelligent under the glow of lamplight—if I hadn't known he was retarded, I would have guessed him to be some junior executive in a bank or even a young superintendent of schools.

By the mid-nineteen sixties, Bryan was beginning to paint some of his best townscapes, and his still lifes were exploding with color. He had reached a point where it was no longer necessary to rely on his mother for technical assistance. In fact, he took pride in his artistic independence, and Mary was immensely pleased when he rejected suggestions. There was, of course, that dependency on his parents for mundane guidance, but he was now his own man at the drawing board and easel.

I must admit an unfairness on my part when viewing his paintings for the first time: they *were* remarkable—I had never seen anything like them—but I couldn't sever my awareness of Bryan's disability and

Mary's efforts to release him from that cage of lifelong helplessness. A nagging conundrum kept rising before me as I stood mesmerized while Mary, too hurriedly, propped one painting after another on an easel. *What if*—I caught myself weighing circumstances—*if* Bryan had been less retarded? Could that nurturing and magic communion between this determined mother and her compliant son have salvaged from a damaged life such talent worthy of acclaim?

I don't recall when the start button on my tape recorder was first pushed forward in Mary's presence—without realizing it, we drifted from polite conversation to a series of in-depth interviews. I do know that she had mixed emotions when granting me permission to write about her son: she liked the idea of Bryan's story appearing in an American publication, though she feared the results would place too great an emphasis on his disabilities and overlook his genuine contributions as a painter.

Some of my questions did nudge the boundaries of privacy, and when these insensitive moments occurred, Mary overlooked them and plunged on while I became the silent captive to extraordinary happenings. Here was a person who had a spontaneous way of recalling the tiniest details and the ability to make these bits and pieces appear as if she were depicting them for the first time.

Mary never missed an opportunity to further her son's career, and this was done while fulfilling the dual roles of protector and publicist. When Bryan went out to draw his townscapes, she often accompanied him. While he drew, she sat close by and made certain that he could work without interruptions. If one of the many tourists inundating picturesque St. Ives seemed genuinely interested in her son's art, a stack of postcard-sized reproductions was quickly brought from her purse. Later, when the two were left alone, she wrote long letters to friends and acquaintances describing Bryan's recent creations and reporting news of coming exhibitions.

Mary knew the value of keeping meticulous records of Bryan's progress, and she was relentless in advancing his work. I am still over-whelmed by the compelling drama of her courage, and I find it difficult to separate his paintings from her presence. Her struggle to do what she felt best for her son brought forth the miracle of Bryan Pearce.

Perhaps he sees, not this world at all,
But something beyond we can't. I met him once
And tried to talk; impossible to gauge
Reactions. He only wants to paint,
To use the one language he has mastered,
But on his terms, his own critique,
Pursuing his soul's vocation.

Lines from the poem *St Ives Bay with Parish Church*
by Donald Rawe, 1980

Mary Pearce grew up in a house overlooking the sea at Carbis Bay, about two miles from the harbor of St. Ives, beyond a cliff path where bungalows were shielded by flourishing gardens.

Her father, Thomas N. Warmington, was highly respected in Cornish music circles for the books of carols and hymns he edited and published. He organized and led the "Carbis Bay Quartet" and played the piano and organ. Mary and her brother, Edward, were frequently surrounded by a choir of voices—it was only later in life that Mary allowed herself the luxury of admitting that she "sometimes grew tired of the sound of sacred music."

T. N. Warmington was not a person who procrastinated—he had no patience for timidity and indecisiveness. At times, when she wavered on a course of action, Warmington would admonish his daughter: "Now look here, Mary, make up your mind! It's either *yes* or *no*; it must be one way or the other!" Years later, after having shared with Walter the burden of making many difficult decisions in the rearing of two handicapped children, she declared: "I owe so much to my father and the way he brought me up to think for myself. Thank God for that!"

Mary's mother was musical—she, too, played the piano and organ— and prior to her marriage Mrs. Warmington had received a diploma in drawing which qualified her to teach. Her interest in painting was passed on to Mary who had plans of attending art school, but before arrangements could be made Mrs. Warmington was taken ill and her daughter's help was needed at home.

Walter's childhood was less sheltered: he was brought up in the center of town, at Market Place, in a household with seven lively brothers. The Pearce family was extremely active in local affairs, and Walter's father had served as Mayor of St. Ives. Rugby was the passion that kept the Pearce boys from being overly competitive at home; they all partici- pated, and four of the brothers, including Walter, played for Cornwall. George, a younger brother, was chosen as a reserve for England.

When Walter began to court Mary, she wondered what possible in- terests, other than dancing and music, the two could share. The Pearce boys were athletes, not the kind to visit museums or sedately stroll the beaches and footpaths. Walter surprised her: he was sensitive to her need to escape the drudgery and responsibilities at home, and his generosity and warmth dispelled all doubts. They were married and began house- keeping at Market Place, in the four-story house that Walter's parents had lived in for many years.

This building had been a public house called The George and Dragon, and for years it was a popular meeting place for the townspeople. Walter's father grew tired of the saloon business and finally converted the street-level rooms into a butcher shop where he and Walter operated a lucrative trade with four employees. Mary, after consulting a local poet, Morton Nance, decided to name the house *Chylowen*, meaning "House of Love" in the extinct Cornish language. She busily began selecting carpets and curtains and spent the first few months of her marriage preparing their new home for the time when they would raise a family.

Bryan Pearce at 10½ months

Their firstborn weighed eight and a half pounds and was christened Walter Bryan. "He's such a sweet little boy and as good as gold," the delighted mother told friends. There were the usual late-night nursing and diaper interruptions that all new parents bear, but it soon became obvious to both Mary and Walter that the baby showed little interest in his surroundings. "Don't worry," Mary was told when she voiced concern, "slow developers move when they are ready."

Walter Bryan sat up at nine months, and to celebrate this joyous occasion, Mary proudly sent a photograph of her son to *A Guide to Care-free Motherhood* hoping that it would be included in the publication's "bonniest babies" column. The picture of the sturdy Bryan with his broad smile was published, but such attention only diverted her concern temporarily.

"He made no effort to crawl or stand up," she recalled, "and Bryan didn't learn to walk until he was nearly two years old. By that time we knew that talking was going to be a problem. When friends of mine stopped by the pram to greet him or hold his little hand, Bryan didn't seem to notice—he just stared into space, as if he wasn't there.

"When he was four, and still unable to speak properly," Mary continued, "we took him to a specialist in London—looking back, all those journeys in search of some doctor to finally help us with both children seemed endless. This specialist told us that it could be a phobia, but as long as he understood that was all that mattered."

There were happenings that somehow slipped through the pulled drapes of Bryan's awareness: his delight at Sabbath gatherings when hymns were sung and when he heard the thunderous call of the church organ. Another fascination was steam engines. Mary spent many hours with her son at the St. Ives railway station so he could watch the arrivals and departures.

"He was so very fond of steamrollers and trains," said Mary. "When Bryan saw them he would shout 'tee-ho! tee-ho!' and start jumping up and down. But if I said 'Yes Bryan, tee-ho,' he would get very angry."

"Then he did know that 'tee-ho' wasn't the correct word for a steamroller or train?" I asked during our first interview.

"It's difficult to realize how much a child does and doesn't understand, but I'm sure he knew. What we didn't know was why he couldn't say it properly."

Walter and Mary pondered the London doctor's comment and tried to be more optimistic when considering their son's chances of living a normal life. Perhaps it *was* some phobia, and it would somehow disappear with the development of new interests or increased activities.

"It was so difficult," Mary told me, "because I didn't know what to do or what was best for him. A hundred times a day he would ask the same question, and I would answer it until I was exhausted and lost all patience. By evening, I would be almost frantic. 'Stop it, Bryan, *stop it*!' I would tell him. 'You *must* not ask that question again!' Then he would kick and scream. It was just pure frustration: Bryan was unable to understand a simple answer to words he couldn't quite express."

"I suppose he had few young people to play with?"

"Only one or two of my friends' children," she answered. "Later, he would come home with bruises on his legs where schoolmates had kicked him or had thrown stones. And I have seen children outside our home calling up 'dafty, dafty!' Bryan would stand at the window, terribly excited, and his hands shaking. He was trying to tell them not to tease him. But he would just stand there, shaking. He didn't have the sense to come away from the window."

"Would his hands shake violently?"

"Oh yes. And he used to go through the streets holding his hands to his ears. I didn't realize then that it was noise that he couldn't stand. I thought it was just one of his queernesses. He would go down at the end of the pier and jump up and down with excitement because from there he could see the train at Porthminster. People used to come and tell me that he was at the edge of the pier. They told me because they were afraid that he would fall in the water and drown. At this time I would have thanked God if he had. For years I prayed that he would fall in. It's a terrible thought now. But there were all the things we had gone through with Bryan; this awful experience of having a fine-looking boy who appeared perfectly normal and bright, and who would say such stupid things which aroused the attention of people around him. I realized that it was better to have Margaretta with her frustration of being unable to speak than it was to have her speaking rubbish. I think the public has more sympathy for a person who can't speak than they have for a person who is mentally handicapped."

The living arrangement at Market Place caused Mary to worry: the steep stairs leading to their quarters above the butcher shop and the roof area where the family washing was hung were danger zones for a solitary and restless child. Walter's mother had brought up eight sons in the house, and not one of them had fallen into the granite causeway below or down the stairway, but the older brothers were able to watch over their younger siblings. On Mary's urging, Walter arranged that a barricade be built by the washroom—a fence that appears in Bryan's 1959 oil *Monday*.

There were advantages in residing at Market Place: the shops, beach and harbor were nearby, and Walter's work was no further than a flight of stairs. Mary, however, felt that Bryan needed more freedom, a holiday retreat where he could run and play safely; some hideaway where they all could be more relaxed. She found it in nearby Hayle—a wooden structure with a little garden and circling paths. "The Better 'Ole," they called it.

Mary had a decorator paint the walls a pale cream, and when the man was unable to find the shade of orange she wanted for the dividing line of the dado, Mary prowled the local shops until she found the color. Even the cream-colored cups and plates were ringed with the same orange, and gingham curtains in checks of red, brown, yellow and orange were selected to enliven the walls. Then, to enhance these warm colors in painterly fashion, she chose green enamel for the cooking pots and teakettle—the interior now had the palette of a future Bryan Pearce.

When seeing the newly-decorated hideaway for the first time, a previously reluctant Walter was eager to spend summers there. In such a setting, Bryan was less restricted—safer, Mary felt; her son could play in the garden and even ride with some coordination his new bicycle along the circling footpaths above the house and shore. During these halcyon days, Mary learned to drive and purchased a little red automobile so she could take Bryan to watch the steam trains at busy Gwinear Road Junction.

It was at this time that the family moved into a new bungalow on a hill not far from the center of town. They called this place *Trelowena,* the Cornish name for "House of Happiness." Even here, Bryan had difficulties, though the Pearce couple did their best to compensate for their son's shortcomings and to shield him from his unsympathetic peers who hooted and kicked him.

"My husband put up an elaborate train set in our new bungalow," Mary recalled, "and for hours Bryan and I would play with that train. I acted as guard and signalman, and he ran the little cars quite well. At times he almost showed good sense, and I was hopeful. Then something would happen, go terribly wrong, and he would get frustrated and cry."

During the nineteen thirties there were few agencies or trained professionals available to parents who had children with learning disabilities. Counseling and support services did exist, though many of the methods for testing mental retardation were still being formulated. The stigma of the word *daft* lingered in the provinces of prejudice. Walter and Mary had to decide for themselves what type of schooling was best for their son, and this was a difficult decision since Bryan was so unpredict-able—he could be calm and compliant one moment, angry and frustrated the next.

Bryan went to nursery school for a short time, and it soon became obvious to the Pearces that he was making no progress. When they learned that he could be enrolled at a boys' boarding school nearby, Mary reluctantly sewed name tags into his new school uniform and with misgivings sent her eight year old away to begin a new life. When the ache of homesickness abated and he became familiar with his new surroundings, Bryan settled in without much complaint.

He did his best to copy the numbers from the blackboard, but his hand was unsteady and his fingers were cramped around the pencil. On the playground, he looked on shyly while his classmates participated in noisy games. The teachers were not impressed with his schoolwork—it was "inferior"—but they all agreed that he "tried hard" in every subject. "He'll probably pick up in his own time," one teacher said when offering encouragement, and Mary held on to that one scrap of hope.

During the second year, at a school event, the headmaster's wife said to her: "I wonder, Mrs. Pearce, if Bryan might be helped by an osteopath? He seems to have a problem with his back and he holds his head down in an odd manner." It was something that had been worrying Mary, and at the end of the term she mentioned it to their family doctor. He immediately dismissed the idea of consulting an osteopath. "It might be best," he told her, "that we send Bryan to see a nerve specialist."

"We took him to London to see two nerve doctors," Mary recalled, "and to a well-known mental specialist. They all advised us to send him to a special school. They said it was the only thing that could help him. We were told that he might get on sufficiently to be able to do a very simple mending job on a pair of shoes. But they gave us no hope."

"Did they say he had phenylketonuria?" I asked.

"Oh no!" she replied. "We didn't know that Bryan had that until eight years ago—when he was thirty years old. All the doctors could tell us then was: 'It's just one of those things.' "

The three experts agreed that there had been brain damage, before or after birth, and the impairment was severe; Bryan would never reach a normal level of intelligence. The Pearces did their utmost to accept the news stoically, but the "shoe mending" image rankled—"no doctor has the right to tell someone there is no chance, no room for hope," she told

Bryan at preparatory school in Cornwall

me, her voice rising. "It's so unfair!"

Before Walter and Mary left London, the specialists did ask why there were no other children. "I told them that we had been afraid to have another child because of Bryan's problems," Mary remembered, "and they assured us that in the history of medicine there had never been more than one like this in a family."

They found a school near London where the care was mainly custodial and the atmosphere seemed serene. His letters home began with short, choppy sentences. "Dear Mummy and Daddy," he would write, "how are you? I am well. How is the harbour? How are the trains?" At times, the words would tumble into a muddle. It happened once at home on holiday when he was writing to his teacher. "Dear Miss Mole," he began, "how are you?" Then there was a plunge into hopeless confusion. "Come quickly," Bryan called out to his mother, "you *must come* help me! All I am writing is rubbish." Mary was concerned but pleased with his self-criticism. Could this be some breakthrough? she wondered.

"Bryan was away from the age of ten to sixteen," she recalled. "This is my one regret in life. I feel he should never have left home. He could talk at this time, but he never told us that he was unhappy. The school was so far away, and he was homesick. It was London and during the war. The school was evacuated first to Hastings, then to Cheltenham, and then to Surrey. It was the time of the flying bombs, and he lived in a shelter for a fortnight. When Bryan came home to stay he told us that he was given little white pills—I suppose it was something to sedate him. Children with phenylketonuria are overactive."

Sometimes the word "school" will ignite memories for Bryan. "If it was a boarding school they would have a trunk like I had," he told his tutor and biographer Marion Whybrow. "Mother sent my trunk in advance by steam train; the Great Western Railway." When asked if he liked school, Bryan replied: "I expect it was all right in its place. Would have been all right if I wasn't homesick—that means not very happy."

Mary Margaretta's birth in 1941 seemed to the delighted parents a portent of happier days. There now would be another family member to help care for Bryan in the future, and this would restore some semblance of order and normalcy to their lives. The new baby squirmed energetically under coverlets. Her blue eyes, fair skin, and light hair drew immediate attention when friends and relatives called on Mary with rattles and knitted clothes. The child nursed hungrily, and the mother marveled at the tiny pink hands curling and uncurling with petal delicacy.

When he could get away from the butcher shop, Walter joined Mary on "airing" excursions along the cobbled streets of St. Ives. The new arrival stared up in wonderment at all who hovered over the carriage to praise the child's softness and glow. "Such a wonderful little one!" strangers would tell the flattered Pearces, and children they didn't even know would follow the pram and call out: "Ain't she a queen, ain't she a beauty—she's ansom, that one!"

When it came time to wean Margaretta, Mary made sure that it was done gradually with spoonfuls of soft cereals, milk and sugar. The six-month-old child had the same good appetite, and no signs of rejection could be detected as new foods were introduced.

"She was bright as a button," said Mary. "Absolutely perfect! But suddenly one day, when I was pushing the pram along the beach road, her little arms and legs became quite rigid and her eyes were glazed as if all life had gone out of them. Then she was seized with tremors that shook her whole body. It was so frightening! I learned later that she was having a petit mal—a minor fit."

The parents tried to calm their fears by bringing up reasonable explanations for the episode; it could have been an allergic reaction—perhaps some food had disagreed with her—or it might have been caused by the cutting of a tooth. They both felt better after a long talk, but soon there were more fits, and several of them were severe.

"We took her to a doctor," Mary recalled, "and he told us to watch her carefully. But the fits gradually got worse, and when she was eleven months old we took her to a London specialist. So there we were, back again with another child, and another worry. It just seemed so endless to us both. We were told that many people went through life with petit mal attacks and were perfectly normal while others had them and were retarded."

"Which couldn't have been very reassuring," I said to her, "after all the difficulties you had with Bryan."

"It was just horrible," she replied, "his telling us not to be too optimistic or too pessimistic. Then at the age of fifteen months we took her again to London because the petit mal seemed heavier, and another specialist prescribed new medicines. These didn't help, and we had to make the best of every day as best we could. Some months later we saw Dr.

Tredgold, a mental specialist, and he said the child never should have been on the medicine we had been given. Dr. Tredgold felt the medication may have damaged her brain and these drugs were only suitable for certain adults. It was at this time we were told our daughter would never talk, never walk."

The Pearces returned home despondent and attempted to resume their lives. Mary took her daughter on daily outings in the pram, cooked meals, scrubbed the floors of the bungalow, shopped, and fought to preserve normalcy; Walter spent long hours at his butcher shop, and made sure that extra money was put aside for medicines and railway fares to visit specialists in London; Bryan, homesick, and sometimes kicked and bullied by classmates at his special school—several years would go by before he told his parents—had no conceivable prospects, and it seemed a certainty that he would be permanently dependent on his family.

At this time Mary began to notice a decline in her own health. It became increasingly difficult for her to lift Margaretta from the bathwater and nearly impossible to wring out the washing or push the pram up a steep hill. She felt dispirited, and there was a definite weakening of willpower when she tried to commandeer her reserves in order to get through another day. More debilitating than poor health was having to bear her daughter's plight—that slow physical deterioration and mental retardation.

When Walter returned home tired after a frustrating day of dealing with wartime ration books and meat shortages in his butcher shop, he would look at Mary and know at a glance whether the baby's fits had been severe that day. There seemed to be no way to circumvent events as the two endured their sorrow and prayed for some miracle to free them from the bondage of disappointment. It was pointless to ask, Walter knew, but both were somehow comforted when a few words were shared. "Was it bad today?" he would ask. "Very bad," she would reply while preparing food for their table.

A small magazine published monthly by the Unity School of Christianity at Unity Village, Missouri, brought some comfort to Mary for a time. The *Daily Word* it was called, and there were messages of hope based on the power of positive thinking and an awareness of the blessings of God. Its tenets were influenced by the theories of Dr. Franz Anton Mesmer, who practiced what was called "animal magnetism." Unity taught a process of healing that used "denial" and mental power. The text of the day offered solace and encouragement, and the message was designed in such a way that it could be enhanced by readings from the Bible. Perhaps a miracle would be bestowed on this child she spoonfed and propped on a pillow. The prospect of her daughter being sentenced to a lifetime of immobility, unthinkable as it was, seemed horribly inevitable.

It was, at times, difficult for Mary to measure her daughter's progress. After weeks of being trained to hold a spoon in her hand, Margaretta was coaxed to bring the utensil to her mouth. Learning to chew and swallow properly took months, and then there was the complication of controlling a napkin. Gradually, one small triumph followed another, and over a period of six years the intricacies of walking and even running and dancing would be mastered.

Mary's mother, Mrs. Warmington, was determined to find some way of helping her grandchild, and also worried that the strain was affecting her daughter's health. "You don't look well," she told Mary one day, and the reply of "How could I be?" deepened concern.

Shortly after this exchange, Mrs. Warmington heard of a "divine healer," a housewife from Kent who was presently in Pendeen, Cornwall. She wrote to the woman asking if a visit to St. Ives was possible—wartime petrol rationing made cross-country journeys difficult. Mary was hostile to the idea. By this time, in spite of the *Daily Word*, she felt there was no hope for Margaretta and even resented the appointment. The healer, a kindly person, who was well aware of the mother's skepticism and understood her anguish, traveled on a bus to St. Ives with two companions.

"Margaretta was three and a half when we had the lady healer sent to us," Mary told me.

"A faith healer?"

I had the distinct feeling that this was one of the few occasions in our long talks when my careless phraseology brought Mary close to the boundary of irritation.

"I don't call them 'faith healers.' These are people who have the gift of healing in their hands."

"This person was not a doctor?"

"Just an ordinary housewife," Mary replied. "At that time, I had no faith that anyone could help Margaretta. I didn't even know how to live a day at a time. I just managed to get through each day, and this is how the three years passed."

"Bryan was attending his special school at this time?"

"Yes," replied Mary. "This woman brought two other ladies with her when she came to our bungalow. Margaretta was on a rug on the floor, and I had cushions around her. 'The little darling!' the lady healer said. 'She's so much better than I expected.' One of the women who came with the healer told me, 'Your child will be better,' and the other added, 'I know she will be better.' I began to think that surely these people must be mad."

"What did the healer do?"

"She administered to Margaretta by manipulating her back, and the lady said that there would be no more fits at the end of three months."

"Was she right?"

"Margaretta was ill with acidosis three and a half months later. I realize now that all the foods I had given both my children were foods they shouldn't have had. Just ordinary foods like eggs, milk and butter. Margaretta couldn't masticate until she was five. I had to spoon the food into her mouth, and she just had to swallow it. This would often cause acidosis. She was very ill for a week, and she had only glucose and water for nourishment. But during that week she had no petit mal attacks. I remember my husband would come home for lunch and ask: 'Well?' I would just shake my head. I couldn't believe that the attacks wouldn't return, and Margaretta didn't have another for six years."

"Did this healer treat your daughter regularly?"

"No. But we had many other people along who helped. It seemed that as soon as one of these people with the gift of healing would leave, another would appear. There was a lady from Africa, a minister from Milton Abbey, a world-leading healer from Liverpool, and a most wonderful old man sent to us from London. When he first came to us he was seventy-nine, and he continued seeing us every six or eight weeks until he was ninety. I feel he really remade both my children's bodies—he was an osteopath with the gift of healing.

"We used to open our home," Mary continued, "and others would come. We have had as many as seventeen people in our bungalow at one time. We would turn our dining room into a surgery, and our lounge into a waiting room. So many wonderful things happened, and so many other people were helped."

Margaretta had been given no chance of a normal life by the several doctors who examined her. She never did talk, but they had also said the child would never walk—this seemed a more terrifying prospect to both Mary and Walter. Now that the fits had ceased, there seemed to be an alertness: their daughter no longer stared blindly at objects. The tiny clenched hands slowly opened like blossoms, and the day she picked up a fallen toffee wrapper was an event never to be forgotten. A step taken, a crayon held, a request heard and fulfilled—these were new skills: miracles!

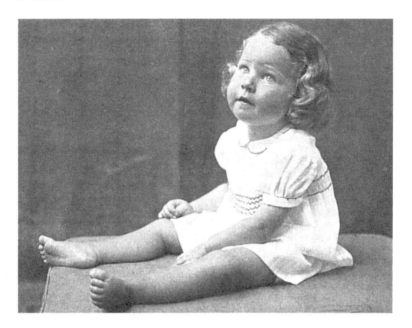

Margaretta at 3¾ years

Margaretta was four and a half before she took her first step; it was obvious that she had no sense of balance and both legs were weak. Slowly, she began to move about with more confidence, though her parents could see that the child needed some sort of support in order to improve mobility. An orthopedist examined Margaretta and she was measured for surgical boots.

Bryan's return from the special school complicated daily routines—there now were increased pressures on Mary as she tried to shield not one, but two handicapped children. They were an odd threesome, she realized, as they paraded along the St. Ives streets: she, neatly attired, convivial, and answering well-meant inquiries—it was difficult to appear cheerful when speaking of her children's progress; there was tiny Margaretta strapped to her stroller, her little boots kicking the metal footrest in a pretend walk; and a shy Bryan, with eyes alert, but his head cast down at an awkward slant.

Walter's good humor and courteous manner drew customers to his butcher shop, and he was particularly popular with young people. Children lost their shyness in his presence—he knew their names and never forgot their interests. When a child was having problems at home or in school, a talk with Walter usually mended matters. The shop at Market Place was also an oasis for Bryan and Margaretta. Walter's young assistant, Dick Peters, played the cornet in the town band, and this alone made him one of Bryan's favorites. Margaretta, in her stroller, squirmed with excitement upon seeing her father, and she responded with a radiant smile when Dick Peters fondly tugged at her curls and played with her fingers.

The Pearces had decided that first and foremost in life they would do their best for Bryan and Margaretta. There would be no room for self-pity; no coddling, no indulging; both children would be disciplined and given the normalcy of rules and restrictions. When Margaretta rebelled, Mary calmed her by focusing the girl's attention on something else in the narrow confines of her world; if this didn't succeed, patience was introduced, and there was always love to help soothe the scrapes and bruises of her fetters.

"When Bryan came home from school," recalled Mary, "I knew he needed to be kept busy—he wasn't the kind to be idle. So I got him to polish the silver and brass. I would watch him carefully and when he didn't do the job properly, I would say, 'Bryan, that won't do, you left some polish in the cracks, it's not good enough.' Then I would sit on a stool in the kitchen while he scrubbed the floor, and when he didn't pay attention I would say, 'No Bryan, you must go over the corners again, there is still grime.' And when the job was done properly, he would look up at me and ask, 'Did I do well?' I would say, 'Yes Bryan, you did very well,' and he would be so proud! His favorite chore was cutting the grass. I even taught him to knit, though sometimes the needles would get crossed and the string would fly off to kingdom come!"

One of Walter's friends was a market gardener, and the kindly man agreed to hire Bryan. Mary was happy for her son, but every morning when he left home eager and willing to work she wondered what misadventure awaited him. It wasn't long before the easygoing gardener became dissatisfied. Bryan did well enough under close and constant supervision, but when left on his own it was soon discovered that the new employee was unable to tell a young plant from a weed.

Home again, he came, and back to Mary. Would he, she worried, ever find some useful work beyond scrubbing floors and polishing brass? A job that was closely supervised and performed with some degree of repetition suited him best. Finally, Walter suggested that Bryan come to the butcher shop—there were always pots and pans to be washed, and in time his son might learn to mince meat and to twist sausages into links.

The parents had instilled in Bryan the importance of being polite, and when he spoke to people his voice was clear and friendly. There was an "old-fashioned courtesy" in his demeanor, a customer told Mary. Music was one of the favorite topics of conversation among the staff at Market Place, and Walter was a member of a choir group. When business was slow, there would be impromptu rehearsals of hymns and Gilbert and Sullivan songs.

Bryan did learn to mince meat and twist sausages into links with some dexterity, and in the convivial surroundings of his father's shop he made friends and had new interests. For Mary, one child less to look after during the daylight hours was a godsend, though she still felt drained and spiritually exhausted. Walter hired women to help his wife with household tasks, and young girls from school came into the home to look after Margaretta. "But they never stayed for long," said Mary, "until Audrey came to us."

A young woman who worked for Walter at Market Place and who was aware of his wife's problems with Margaretta, suggested that her sister, Audrey, might be of some help to Mary. The girl was fourteen and slowly recovering from a serious illness. She wasn't strong enough to do heavy work but would be able to take Margaretta for her daily excursions in the pram.

"Audrey was a shy, dark-haired girl who was with us for nearly fourteen years," Mary recalled, "and she became in every way a member of our family. I don't know what I would have done without her. 'Audrey' was the only word our daughter ever spoke. The two were playing at the shore one day and Audrey came up from behind a rock and startled Margaretta. 'Audrey!' she called out in such a clear and surprised voice. But it was only that one time."

Margaretta was outgoing and eager to meet people. She was her brother's opposite: bold instead of shy, aggressive instead of withdrawn—she never lost her cheerfulness or courage when challenged by problems. The inability to speak isolated her, and she had the disadvantage of being unsteady on her feet throughout much of her early childhood. At home, the little one staggered from room to room in search of new adventures.

"Our daughter knew all the nursery rhymes by heart," said Mary, "and if anyone got a word out of place reading to her, she would shout or make some gesture to let us know that she resented the mistake. Margaretta didn't care two hoots for anybody or anything, and being unable to speak made little difference—she would just drag and pull at us and make noises."

Ruth Jones, in her Bryan Pearce biography, *The Path of the Son*, 1976 and 1993, wrote that "Walter's homecoming in the evening was the highlight of Margaretta's day, and from the privileged safety of her father's knee, she felt that she was mistress of all she surveyed." The little girl's "blue eyes were clear and bright with long dark lashes that brushed against the soft peach roundness of her cheeks. Walter, looking down at her rosy face and fine golden hair, felt at times the happiest father alive."

Mary regarded her daughter's spontaneity and inclinations to be aggressive and stubborn as bonuses, but when the child misbehaved she was disciplined. There were few guidelines for bringing up a handicapped little one, and Mary decided a commonsense approach would be best. When the command "hang up your coat" went unheeded, all pleasures were postponed. In the beginning, if it took an hour before the cloth found its hanger, both Mary and Audrey had patience and time to wait. Eventually, toys were put away properly, the room picked up, and Margaretta learned when to wash her hands and face.

Mary taught her daughter how to set a table by creating a board with cutout shapes of dishes and utensils. "But she could be contrary," said Mary. "Margaretta would hover over the board with a piece ready to fit into its proper place and look up at me with the cheekiest of smiles and move it carefully onto a different shape. I felt sure that one day there would be a breakthrough. She seemed so close to understanding every-thing. Still, it was such a relief some days to see Audrey pushing the stroller out of sight and I could have a little time away from my daughter."

On these outings down the beach road past the harbor and through the cobbled streets, Margaretta was intensely alert and the slightest hap-pening woke her radiant smile. If the wind was gusting in from the sea and boats were tossing and seagulls complaining, the child would call out and wave excitedly. Audrey was still not robust enough to push the stroller up the slope to the bungalow so Mary kept watch and came down the hill to help them home.

"Margaretta was growing faster than Audrey was getting back her strength," recalled Mary, "and this worried me. I prayed every day that there would come a time when I could take my daughter's hand and walk with her on the beach and through the streets."

When the elderly osteopath first called on the Pearces, Margaretta was seven years old and still reeling about the bungalow in surgical boots. "We must dispense with these immediately, Mrs. Pearce," he told her. She burned the boots in the kitchen boiler; they had cost more than eight pounds—a laborer might toil two weeks to earn such a sum. But for Mary this was no rash act: "I had to believe what that wonderful old man told me."

A pair of "trim new shoes and smart white socks" were brought home for Margaretta, and the child put them on with "big eyes and trembling gestures." Mary never forgot how feminine her daughter appeared in those new shoes, "but when I looked closely at her fragile little legs, I almost regretted having burned the boots."

Nearly a year went by before Margaretta stopped dragging her feet, and eventually Mary's dream of accompanying her daughter on long walks was realized. The stroller was discarded on the day that the child was able to climb the cliff path at Carbis Bay. There now were beach picnics, outings in nearby Zennor, and when Margaretta's coordination improved noticeably, Mary arranged dancing lessons at home with a Mrs. Nance. "That girl is naturally graceful," the teacher told a delighted mother.

There were few chances for Walter and Mary to enjoy themselves to-gether and to get away from the obligations of parenthood, but with Audrey in charge at home, the two were able to spend Wednesday eve-nings dancing at the town hall. Mary wore her prettiest clothes, mingled with old and new friends, and felt almost carefree as she and Walter circled the dance floor.

"It was different at home," she declared when recalling that period in her life. "Sometimes during those long evenings with my husband tired from work and dozing in his chair, Margaretta finally in bed, and Bryan listening to records in his room, I would sit by the fire and think of the past and wonder what kind of a future was in store for us. 'Can this be happening,' I would ask myself, 'that my daughter, sleeping so innocently, will never speak, will never enter into the everyday world, and that Bryan, now so engrossed in his music, will never be able to manage things for himself?' "

Walter shared his wife's apprehensions, though his role was principally that of breadwinner and protector of the family. He did live trustingly from day to day and had available a reservoir of strength and humor. Mary kept her anxieties under control, and some of Walter's concerns were eased by the distraction of running his butcher shop. He also had cronies to sustain him when the outlook at home seemed bleak. As a couple, the Pearces found the necessary courage, spirit, and faith to make acceptable, and sometimes even enjoyable, the troubled lives they led.

Bryan was now twenty and still a devoted steam train watcher. One of his greatest joys was being taken to see the tank engines at Long Rock. Mary would make the journey in her little red automobile, Bryan sitting proudly up front and a lively Margaretta in the backseat. When they drove down the familiar road to Long Rock, the little girl would burst into her wordless rendition of "The railway train is starting off"— a tune that Granny Warmington often played for her on the piano. Margaretta sounded it so triumphantly that Mary was encouraged by her daughter's spontaneous flair of intelligence. Could the breakthrough be near?

All outdoor activities attracted Margaretta. Her leg muscles now were strong and she loved running barefoot on the beach and feeling the wind in her hair. One day at home she was running and fell; this time she didn't return to her feet laughing. The doctor examined her and told the frantic mother that it was another fit. "From then on she had them for the rest of her life," said Mary. "But now the attacks were grand mal."

In spite of the difference in their ages—Bryan born in 1929, Margaretta in 1941—sibling rivalry erupted as the younger one became more curious and physically active. The "big brother" role had little appeal for Bryan as Margaretta disturbed his prized possessions and teased him to get attention. He felt threatened when daily routines were interrupted, and at times showed little patience for his sister's exuberance. Rooms of their own were needed, Mary realized, and boundaries established to stimulate development and to preserve harmony. She had the builders come, and two new rooms were added to the bungalow.

Brother and sister had their differences in music. Bryan preferred hymns and classical compositions and Margaretta adored the carefree Gilbert and Sullivan recordings, particularly *The Mikado*. She found her brother's choices tiresome and took impish delight in nudging the gramophone arm when Bryan was playing one of his favorites. My turn, she would gesture, holding up one of her rowdy selections. Later, approaching womanhood, Margaretta's first choice became "I'm Getting Married in the Morning"—from *My Fair Lady*. The irony of circumstance as her happy daughter swayed in step while reaching out for words that would never come saddened the concerned mother.

Bryan's interest in hymns manifested itself as early as eighteen months, when his parents took him to chapel, and he responded with increased enjoyment throughout childhood. Music might well have been his life had there been no brain damage. "It was one of the few things that Bryan and his sister had in common," Mary told me in an early interview. "Our daughter had a wonderful voice—so much so that she could almost sing the words!"

Bryan had now won for himself some independence: he had his private space and music from a sizeable collection of records, he could make his own bed, and every workday morning he and his father left the bungalow for the butcher shop—Bryan so proud of his shined shoes and glistening white shirt.

When asked to describe her daughter, the first word that came to Mary was "sport"—that seemed to accurately categorize Margaretta's radiant personality, her energy, and enthusiasm. With these qualities in mind, and eager to find new outlets for their daughter, Walter and Mary decided that she should be given horse-riding lessons. They took her to a farm on the moors behind St. Ives where two women taught horsemanship. The moment Margaretta was helped onto the back of a docile mare the girl began to laugh uncontrollably until she wept. "We were all astonished," recalled Mary, "and later it was just wonderful to watch her. She learned to ride with such ease and grace."

Bryan disliked every moment of his onetime adventure as an equestrian. He sat stiffly in the saddle and tightly gripped the reins. Mary recalled how differently her two children had reacted when they were pushed in a swing on the playground: Margaretta loved the motion, and the higher she rose in the air the more she laughed and screamed with excitement; Bryan approached the contraption with suspicion, held on solemnly, and dragged his feet on the ground when he was pushed briskly.

Brother and sister were opposites in their reactions and attitudes. Bryan would walk carefully along the streets, keeping a safe distance from traffic, his head down, and only occasionally would he allow himself a shy and diagonal glance upward. If someone spoke to him, he would slow his purposeful steps and ration pleasantries. At times, his behavior in public was eccentric—my wife and I have seen him tracing the texture of walls with his fingers in passing while muttering some dispute with himself just over his breath.

Margaretta's parade through the streets of St. Ives turned heads in admiration. She was exceptionally pretty, and there was a carefree bounce to her step which expressed trust and confidence. The girl had no fear of traffic and often flirted with danger. Mary and Audrey were always in pursuit as she pranced her haphazard way to the harbor.

The butcher shop gave Bryan an opportunity to mingle with employees and to have brief conversations with customers. He did his work slowly and with utmost care: mincing the meats, scrubbing pans and floors, and keeping the butcher block immaculate were routines to be taken seriously. Mary, however, felt there should be more in life for her son than these repetitive chores, and this opinion was shared by her mother, Mrs. Warmington, who had spent months teaching her grandson to play a few simple tunes on the piano. Her efforts to give him a more meaningful outlet failed because of his inability to read music. Bryan, in spite of his accurate ear, could not reach the level of competence he envisioned; his desire to become an accomplished musician was a hopeless dream, and this failure upset him.

"How did Bryan get interested in painting?" I asked Mary.

"When he was very small," she replied, "his father would draw little pictures of tank engines for him, and Bryan would draw them too. So my mother said to me one day, 'I wonder why you don't take Bryan to one of the artists to see if he can paint or draw?' I told my mother that I had asked him several times, but he never seemed interested. She suggested that I ask him again. So later I said to him, 'Now Bryan, I'm going to ask you a question, and I want you to think about it before you answer me. Would you like me to take you to one of the artists to see if you can draw or paint?' And he said to me, 'No thank you. My only desire is to play the organ in The Albert Hall.' "

"Where did he get that idea?" I asked.

"I suppose from some recording of music," replied Mary. "What an ambition! But my mother said, 'Go to Woolworth's and get him a drawing book. Don't give up!' I went and bought one. In the book there was a picture of a cornet in bright yellow, and on the opposite page the black outlines. I fetched a box of watercolors and a mug of water, put them on the kitchen table and called him. 'I thought you could paint this lovely cornet! Dick plays the cornet'—he was one of the fellows in the butcher shop. 'Wouldn't you like to paint this?' I think because it was a musical instrument he became interested. He painted it beautifully and was so delighted. This was how it all started."

Audrey and his father praised this first attempt with the paintbrush, but when he showed the picture to his sister she quickly turned away. Margaretta was convinced that her wild scrawls on paper deserved more attention.

Mary knew she had to approach her son cautiously; at twenty-four and set in his ways, Bryan usually resisted change—he preferred routine chores and found safety in repetition. Ever so gently, she nudged him into painting some of the other pictures in the book, and before his interest waned, Mary brought home seaweed and shells from the beach. He drew coloring-book outlines of these and brightened them as if they were cornets. Fruit and branches from the garden were introduced next as subject matter, and to her surprise Bryan willingly accepted these challenges.

"Did he have any art lessons prior to his attending the St. Ives School of Painting?"—This was one of the questions I had asked Mary during the first of our interview sessions.

"He did little bits and pieces of odd things I gave him to paint," she replied, "and one day Isobel Heath, who is a painter, came into my husband's shop. Bryan was there, and jokingly, Walter said to her, 'I think we're going to have an artist in the family, Miss Heath.' Then he told her that Bryan had been painting. 'Are you really interested?' she asked him. And he replied, 'I think I am—a bit.' "

Isobel Heath's kindliness and her ability to appreciate the works of fellow artists from a wide spectrum of approaches were qualities which helped Bryan enormously during the brief period he spent with her. Heath had studied art in Paris and at the St. Ives School of Painting. During World War II, she worked for the Ministry of Information, and one of her duties was making sketches of factory workers. Miss Heath had been a member of the St. Ives Society of Artists and then joined the splinter group that formed the Penwith Society of Arts in Cornwall in 1949. The following year she resigned when a controversy arose over the categorizing of abstract and representational artists.

"She had Bryan come to her studio once a week for three months," said Mary, "and I would occasionally ask her how he was doing. 'He's got something, you know,' she would reply, and I would say to Walter: 'What on earth has he got?' When I saw those first little things I wondered how she could say that he had anything—it just puzzled us both.

"After three months," continued Mary, "Miss Heath was going away on holidays and she came to me and told me that I must take Byran to Leonard Fuller at the St. Ives School of Painting. But I felt I couldn't possibly ask him—I had to deny my son so many things over the years because of his handicap. Miss Heath insisted and wrote a note to Mr. Fuller, and when I went to see him, he said, 'Certainly Bryan can come to me.' I couldn't believe this was happening!"

Leonard Fuller's St. Ives School of Painting was established in April 1938. He had been invited to visit Cornwall by seascape painter Borlase Smart, a World War I friend, and liking the area Fuller settled in St. Ives. The school was located at 11 Porthmeor Studios, Back Road West—just a few doors from the small cottage where seventy-year-old primitive artist Alfred Wallis began painting on cardboard "for company" after the death of his wife. Fuller, trained as a portrait painter, had taught drawing at St. John's Wood Art Schools and Dulwich College in London. Over the years, hundreds of students—many of whom became established artists—have benefited from his instructions in the traditional arts of drawing and painting.

One afternoon while I was visiting Misomé Peile at her studio, an unfinished work in a sketchbook nudged my attention. It was simply done, just a room with unpolished boards and high ceiling. A pale sky was framed in the window that lighted a figure standing before an easel. This, I was told, was an interior sketch completed while Misomé was attending Mr. Fuller's classes.

The students were of all ages, and during the winter months the emphasis was on the basic techniques of painting. Still lifes, interiors, and portraits reigned, and Fuller was able to hire a number of attractive girls in the neighborhood as models. Boisterous discussions followed instructions, and everyone "huddled round an old black stove which was the only pitiful source of heat." The roof leaked, and at times the smell of turpentine was overpowering. Painting outside was scheduled on warm and sunny days, and Fuller's students were delighted when they could escape their "old-fashioned surroundings." The narrow streets were crowded with resident artists, and there were many vantage points where one could set up an easel or drawing board.

Bryan was twenty-four when he entered the St. Ives School of Painting, and it was arranged that he attend classes four mornings a week. Leonard Fuller was pleased with his new student's meticulous work habits and his willingness to begin assignments, though the first drawings and watercolors were done with little control. An early study of the Porthmeor studio showed furnishings that reminded one of a fleet of small boats in a boiling sea: the tables and chairs were listing precariously along a wavy floor.

Fuller realized that Bryan understood little of what was being said in classroom discussions; it was more important to provide the right environment in which the young man could work at his own deliberate pace—some thoughtless comment or the suggestion of altering a line would only lead to confusion and loss of confidence.

"Mr. Fuller was very kind," declared Mary. "He used to take him out with a little table and chair to the back alleys and down at the harbor where Bryan would sit and paint his watercolors. You can tell by those early paintings that his hands were shaking badly, and when the wind would blow up, some kindly person would come and tie a piece of string around a stone to weight the paper down.

"I used to go to Mr. Fuller every so often to see how Bryan was doing," she recalled. "I realized he was there with the other students and wondered if he was saying silly things. Mr. Fuller told me: 'If every student of mine worked as hard as Bryan, I would be a happy man! I take him out and place him at his little table, and whatever time of the morning I go back, I'll find him there still working.' "

Mary found this comment comforting, though there were threads of doubt lingering from past experiences: was he being exposed to the same ridicule, the same thoughtless remarks? She frequently wondered what people said when they saw him at his table, head down at a slant, and hands shaking. "Did anyone speak to you today, Bryan?" she would ask, trying to hide her concern. "Only that nice lady with the glasses and gray hair," he would say matter-of-factly. His reply was casual enough to be reassuring; maybe he *was* beginning a life on his own and making new contacts.

"What on earth is he doing now, Mrs. Pearce?" Leonard Fuller asked her one day.

"Why don't you ask him?"

"I have," he replied, "and he said it was Hayle Harbor."

She went over to Bryan's table and studied the intricate grid of lines that her son had set out on paper. It took time to find a familiar land-mark but once that was established everything fell into place: the har-bor scene Bryan had planned was aerial in perspective—from memory he had arranged bridges, docks, and boats in a circle. Even the signal beside a railway line was horizontally rendered, and the houses were compressed and distorted to fit his rectangular sheet of drawing paper.

"Oh yes," Mary told Fuller, "it's Hayle Harbor."

"It looks like a map," he said, not fully understanding Bryan's overall design.

"I suppose it does—a bit," she admitted.

"One side is right and three sides are wrong," he said, amused and bewildered by the thought.

Walter's butcher shop flourished with the increase of holiday visitors to St. Ives, and the business was less frustrating now that rationing and wartime restrictions were no longer necessary. The two rooms added to the bungalow gave Bryan and Margaretta more space and freedom to pursue their interests, and with Audrey in charge, Mary had time for herself during the daylight hours, though her nights were still spent in and out of restless sleep. Too often, Mary thought she heard the first telltale sounds of another grand mal seizure in the next room.

Margaretta was totally unaware of her precarious health, and had she known, the girl probably would have responded with a shrug, much as

MONDAY, 1959, Oil on board 22 x 30 ins., Collection: Artist

NON-FLOWERING BEGONIA & FRUIT, 1960
Oil on board 30 x 21 ins., Private Collection

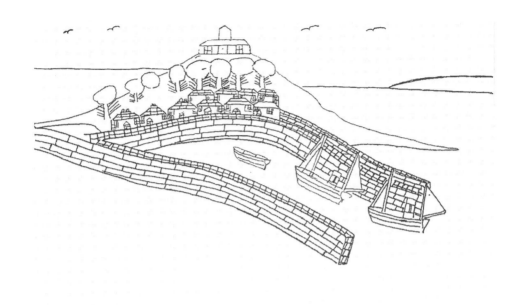

Bryan Pearce

ST MICHAEL'S MOUNT, 1965, Pen and ink 12 x 18 ins., Collection: C. J. Stevens

Bryan Pearce

ST JUST-IN-ROSELAND, 1971, Oil on board 22 x 28 ins., Private Collection

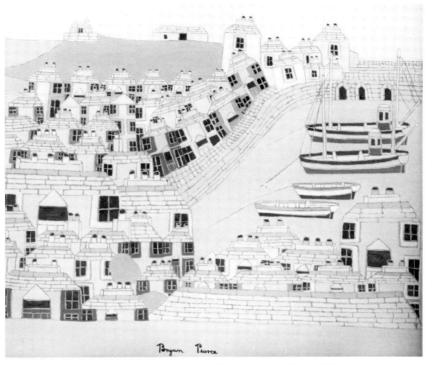

ST IVES FROM BARNOON TERRACE, 1972
Oil on board 20 x 24 ins., Private Collection

TEA CADDY AND GOURDS, 1972, 20 x 16 ins., Private Collection

TOWEDNACK CHURCH (INTERIOR), 1972
Oil on board 24 x 20 ins., Private Collection

THREE FISHING BOATS, 1972, 16 x 20 ins., Private Collection

THE MANOR HOUSE (PRE-1646), 1973
Oil on board 20 x 24 ins., Private Collection

RED GLOXINIA ON BLUE CLOTH, 1973, 24 x 20 ins., Private Collection

THE MEADOW, ST IVES, 1974, Oil on board 20 x 24 ins., Private Collection

THE ISLAND FROM PIAZZA, ST IVES, 1974, 20 x 24 ins., Private Collection

ST IVES HARBOUR (ALL ROUND), 1991, 22 X 28 ins., Private Collection

COFFEE POT by Mary Pearce, 1960

she did when being restrained from dashing recklessly into busy inter-
sections. She was spirited and carefree; her growing feminine appeal
meant nothing to her—she had no interest in the pretty clothes that Mary
spent hours choosing for her.

Bryan insisted on a bandbox appearance and rushed to his mother in
distress when he found the smallest smudge on a suit. Scuffed shoes
were never placed in his closet without being shined, and they had to be
lined up in soldierly formation. Mary recalled with amusement Bryan's
impatience one day when his father clumsily attempted to help him knot
a stubborn necktie.

There was time set aside for leisure: Mary hired a canvas enclosure
so the family could enjoy picnic meals together at Porthmeor Beach.
When sympathetic relatives joined the Pearces, Bryan and Margaretta
were less likely to be stared at by insensitive beachgoers. Sometimes,
these summer visitors would turn their deck chairs away from the sea in
order to watch the hyperactive antics of the young girl who would never
speak. Bryan's solemn composure allowed him to escape much of this
unwanted attention; it was only when his "Mommy-and-Daddy" remarks
were overheard that stares were turned in his direction.

"Little things," I heard Mary say, "wore me down."

She could never get Bryan to go swimming when they went to the
beach: he preferred to join the family fully clothed or to sit by himself in
the shade. Without supervision, Margaretta would have been horribly
sunburned or thrashing helplessly in deep water. At times, Mary de-
spaired and saw no chance of her two children behaving with any degree
of normalcy or being accepted by their peers. She wondered if there
would come a time, in the years ahead, when she could not afford to die;
that her role in life was to elevate and to defend them forever; and most
of all, did she have the courage and strength to shoulder this task?

Lack of sleep and the fear that Margaretta's grand mal incidents would
increase in severity caused a general decline in Mary's health. Walter
was concerned, and after much persuading he got her to seek medical
advice. She must "work less and worry less," the doctor counseled; he
suggested that the steep hill to their bungalow was a strain on her heart,
and recommended a place situated on level ground.

They first resisted the idea of leaving *Trelowena.* The bungalow had
been their sanctuary for nearly twenty years, and it was here that the
healers had come to perform their many miracles. The two additional

rooms were so ideally suited for their children's needs, and *Trelowena* had been Margaretta's only home.

After lengthy discussions they decided that a return to Market Place was the inevitable solution, and Mary arranged with the builders to have the old staircase entrance sealed off and a new one made at the back of the house on more level ground. Here in fortresslike surroundings of thick walls, large rooms and broad windows, the Pearces felt more secure: somehow, imperceptibly, the bungalow had made them feel more vulnerable to outsiders. There were many kind and caring acquaintances in the vicinity, but friendly visits to *Trelowena* carried an aura of a conducted tour to "see poor Mary."

Walter's mother lived at Eden House—which was nearby—and his brothers and cousins, very sociable and influential in town affairs, were frequent callers at Market Place. Walter, so close to his work, had more time at home; Bryan and Margaretta loved being teased and spoiled by uncles and aunts; and Mary enjoyed being at the center of all this activity—"there were no more long hauls up that hill," she remarked, "and Audrey and Margaretta could easily do their shopping or go to the library."

The resident artists in St. Ives had long followed the custom of holding an "Annual Show Day" in order to acquaint the local people with what was being done in the various studios and to attract potential customers. It also was an opportunity for Leonard Fuller to exhibit the work of his students and to promote his school.

Bryan's watercolors—and certainly Bryan—were of special interest to many people in town. Several of his small paintings were displayed on a large sheet of paper, and Mary lingered in the background intent on overhearing what was being said about her son's work.

"After the show," she recalled, "Mr. Fuller came to me and said that someone wanted to buy one of Bryan's little watercolors—a picture of an old couch. I asked, 'Who on earth wants that!' He said it was Dorothy Bordass, an artist from the Far East who had just returned to St. Ives. I remember asking him if he thought half a crown would be too much. 'Oh,' he said, 'I think you could ask five shillings.' That was the first picture Bryan sold."

Several artists at the St. Ives School of Painting found purchasers that day, but no sale received more attention than the watercolor of

Bryan's old couch. At home, Walter and Audrey were extremely amused to hear that he had found a buyer, and at the butcher shop Bryan was cheered for his good fortune.

"A few days later," Mary continued, "I met the lady, and she said to me, 'Your son should never be at Mr. Fuller's. He should be left entirely alone because Bryan is a genuine primitive.' I went straight to Mr. Fuller and told him. We talked and he agreed to let Bryan come to his school to paint and he promised not to instruct him. I think Mr. Fuller found this arrangement difficult, and it was very good of him. I was going there two mornings a week and was able to guard him and to see that nothing was said. Bryan could have been ruined completely or his work could have been just mediocre if there had been instructions."

Mary Pearce, July 1956

"I had wanted to paint all my life," Mary told me, "but there was always something for me to do. First, there was my mother to look after for years, and when I got married there were the children. We moved from our bungalow to Market Place during the time that Bryan was at

Mr. Fuller's, and I felt it would be so easy for me to go there myself. So I drew for one term, and I used to go twice a week."

It was a new world for Mary, and some of her cherished memories were of that brief time at the St. Ives School of Painting. No student followed the lessons more closely, and she particularly enjoyed the discussions with Mr. Fuller after classes when he reviewed individual work habits and problems.

Fuller was delighted with Mary's progress in portrait painting—her likenesses rivaled and often surpassed anything done in his classes, but the way she achieved resemblances astonished him. He had never witnessed such a singular approach: there were no preliminary studies, no outlines, and most puzzling was her straightforward method of beginning a painting without hesitation. She concentrated on the area above the eyes during the first lessons; for the next sittings she moved down to the central third of the face and then she completed the portrait by painting the mouth, chin, and neck. These eccentricities bewildered Fuller, though there was no denying results—her colors were sensitively chosen, and they seemed to explode with freshness.

Mary soon realized that she needed more time to paint; two classes a week at Mr. Fuller's were not enough, and at Market Place there was no quiet alcove or room away from the family to set up a makeshift studio.

"There *was* an old storeroom in the attic," Mary recalled, "and we had a large window put in for extra light. You could see the rooftops of the town from the high window. It was so wonderful, and this was the first space I ever had for myself—I was all alone up there with my easel, drawing board, and paints."

She began by completing several still lifes, and her careful technique was demonstrated in flower paintings—she slowly brought forth these blossoms petal by petal into a harmonious whole. But the work was interrupted by a curious Bryan who toured his mother's domain.

"I like the window," he told her.

"Yes Bryan. One can see all the rooftops."

No more was said during that first visit, and soon he was coming regularly.

"When are you going to hang some of my pictures?" he asked one day.

Mary hung two on her studio wall.

"When are you going to hang more?" he asked on another visit.

"So I hung four," said Mary. "By that time there wasn't much room for mine. So it became his studio, and I moved to the front of our house to paint. Bryan didn't go to Mr. Fuller's after he had his own studio at home."

Her son usually said little about his paintings, though there were occasions when he sought his mother's opinion. He had just begun working in oils, and it was obvious that he possessed a natural instinct for blending colors.

"I've finished my painting," he announced. "Do you like it?"

"Well, yes Bryan, it's very nice," she replied.

There was, however, a slight shading of disapproval in her voice.

"Do you really like it?" he tried again, this time hopeful of being accorded Mary's usual enthusiasm when viewing his work.

The little oil he had completed was not among his better efforts, and his mother felt it had few merits. Instead of criticizing the painting, she decided to spare his feelings by focusing his attention on something else.

"Well," she said, producing one of her recent still lifes for inspection, "what do you think of mine?"

Bryan marched over to where she had propped her painting on a chair, looked at it briefly, and with the loftiness of a stern but kindly art master, he turned toward his mother and said, "Well, it's near enough."

"In the beginning," I wondered, "Wasn't painting just something to keep him occupied?"

"It was never more than that," Mary replied. "I think we began to realize that he had something special after he started painting at home. Some of the students and teachers at Mr. Fuller's had told me how much they liked his work. I thought they were just being kind. But one day I plucked up my courage and asked several of them if they would come to our home and see his work. They came and said so many wonderful things that I began to feel that there must be something in it."

With a studio of his own, Bryan now spent most of the day working. There was no need for him to experiment or to plan a picture; he just went ahead, entirely confident. Each brush stroke was placed deliberately, and the pace neither quickened nor became uneven because of mood or impulse. When his mother visited with morning coffee or called him for meals, she always found him leaning forward in a nearsighted crouch as if he "wanted to crawl into the picture."

Soon, his own method of developing a painting evolved, and nothing seemed to escape his attention as he impartially assigned each tile, window, street and flower to its inevitable place within the confines of a canvas.

Mary never knew what to expect when she brought Bryan some fruit, vegetable, or dish for a still life. Under his care, leaves exploded with veins, and stems of flowers in glass vases crystallized into magnified life. His potted plants rioted with such vibrancy that often her earlier artistic concept of them had to be reassessed. "Now what on earth will Bryan make of these?" she frequently asked herself when going up the stairs to his studio.

When still lifes caused him to grow restless, he returned to townscapes. The houses along Barnoon Hill were an alluring background for his black windows and rusty rooftops, and so were the trees in the garden of sculptor Barbara Hepworth's *Trewyn*—these he rendered as decorative green globes on sturdy trunks.

Mary missed having a studio of her own, and after several distracting weeks of family activity and a restless Margaretta she "teased" Walter into having the builders come and convert the unused attic area at the front of the house. When the tiles were removed from the rafters and a window installed, the Pearces were awestruck by the magnificent view sweeping before them—the waters of the bay could be seen from Clodgy Point in the west to the island lighthouse of Godrevy. It didn't take long for Bryan to utilize this scene of crowded houses and slanting rooftops, the skyline of Hayle, and boats in the harbor for another series of St. Ives townscapes.

Mary turned away from the incredible view and concentrated on furthering her careful stylistic approach in several new still lifes and flower paintings. Occasionally, Bryan would call out to ask her advice on what color to use or how some huddle of houses should be placed on a canvas. But she could see he was becoming more independent and often her opinions were swiftly rejected.

One picture after another had been stored by Mary in wooden racks under the eaves of Bryan's attic studio, and gradually she accumulated a collection of her son's work varied and large enough to reveal his style and development. It was now obvious to Mary that more people should see his paintings.

Someone suggested that she try the Penwith Society of Arts. This group had a gallery in Fore Street and encouraged new and unconventional styles of paintings. The membership also had established a lay member exhibition which seemed ideally suited for Bryan.

"The person at the Penwith Gallery told me that his work was acceptable," said Mary, "but I would have to have a sponsor to show there. I didn't know many artists in those days—we had kept to ourselves so much because of our children. The only person I could think of was Mr. Fuller. So I went to him and asked if he would sponsor Bryan for the Penwith. He said, 'No, Mrs. Pearce, not yet. I really don't think he is ready.' I was horrified! I could have wept, and it made me angry. I was hurt—terribly! I just marched out. The only other person I could think of was Denis Mitchell, the sculptor. After Mr. Fuller's refusal, I was more determined than ever. So I went to him. 'Certainly, Mrs. Pearce,' he said. 'I have seen your son's work and I like it very much indeed.' So he came to the studio and picked out five of Bryan's paintings, and they were sent to the Penwith Gallery for their 1957 exhibit."

The paintings were favorably received at the Penwith showing, and in an October 1957 issue of *The St. Ives Times and Echo* Wendy Oliver described Bryan's work as that of a "true primitive." His *Blue Jar and Fruit*, 1957, was for Oliver "so complete, so free from inessentials that it makes other good paintings look finicky and overworked."

Mary was delighted with this first public assessment of her son's work, and Bryan smiled when his mother explained to him the significance of the write-up, though she could tell that it meant very little to him. During his Penwith outing Bryan walked around the gallery with noticeable embarrassment, and when he came near his own paintings he shyly glanced at them and moved on.

At the turn of the twentieth century, St. Ives was a busy fishing port with a fleet of more than a hundred sailing boats, and fishermen made a comfortable annual income by working on a share basis. Then came the large steam trawlers that cleared the waters of fish and spawns. The St. Ives sailing boats were no competition for these giant vessels, and when local crews had a good catch, the markets, under the control of larger firms, offered pittance, and the fish had to be thrown back into the sea.

Before tourism replaced fishing as an industry, the activities of painters aroused suspicion in St. Ives. When Louis Grier set up his easel along the wharf—this was on a Sunday—Grier was quickly told by one observer to clear out and if he didn't he and his easel would be pitched into the harbor. A story summing up the general attitude locals had for painters tells of a horse that refused to climb Skidden Hill. The angry driver let loose a barrage of cusswords, and finally, after exhausting his colorful and extensive vocabulary, he jumped from his stalled conveyance, grabbed the recalcitrant animal by its halter, and shouted, "You—you bloody artist!"

St. Ives has long been a desirable location for painters with its circle of beaches, intriguing maze of alleyways and cobbled streets, and in recent years with the establishment of the Tate Gallery St. Ives it is regarded as one of the leading art centers. Among the first artists to visit West Cornwall were Joseph Turner in 1811 and Walter Sickert and James McNeill Whistler in the 1880s. The good light of St. Ives and Newlyn proved irresistible for both the professional and amateur, which led to the emergence of art galleries and thriving groups of painters. The St. Ives Arts Club was established in 1890, and in 1927 the St. Ives Society of Artists was founded and began to hold exhibitions. Painters at their easels were a common sight around town and part of the picturesque backdrop for summer tourists.

Conventional art reigned until World War II when constructionist artist, designer, writer and teacher Naum Gabo helped to precipitate the rejection of traditional styles and became one of the leading exponents for the modern movement in St. Ives, along with Ben Nicholson, Barbara Hepworth, and potter Bernard Leach.

Nicholson first visited Cornwall in 1928 when he and painter Christopher Wood attended an exhibition being held by the St. Ives Society of Artists. "On the way from Porthmeor Beach," recalled Nicholson, "we passed an open door in Back Road West and through it saw some paintings of ships and houses on odd pieces of paper and cardboard nailed up all over the wall, with particularly large nails through the smallest ones." Upon entering, they found an elderly painter at work, "looking," according to Wood, "just like Cézanne."

It is doubtful whether Alfred Wallis or Bryan Pearce would have taken up painting as an outlet had they lived in some other area. While Wallis was working on a fishing boat out of Newlyn, its art colony was active, and when he moved to St. Ives there were painters at their easels along the harbor and in the backstreets. Their presence must have had some influence on his decision to do "a bit of paintin'. "

Wallis's primitivism captivated the two callers that day, though it is impossible to measure the extent of his influence over them, in light of Nicholson's complex abstract compositions and the tragedy of Wood's early death by suicide in 1930.

"No village or small town that I know of anywhere has had so strong an appeal as St Ives," wrote Bernard Leach, "and no small place has become so widely known through the work of its artists." Publicity in national magazines drew attention to both painter and community, and many individuals whose work might have been ignored elsewhere found sanctuary in the art colonies of St. Ives and Newlyn. The modern movement brought forth by Gabo, Nicholson, Hepworth, and the presence of Bernard Leach's pottery on the outskirts of St. Ives were inducements enough to fuse a cultural explosion. The great divide between open-air versus studio painting now became a rift between abstract and representational art.

Among those who had resigned their membership in the St. Ives Society of Artists and joined a group of "moderns" to form the Penwith Society of Arts in Cornwall in 1949 were Isobel Heath, Misomé Peile, and Shearer Armstrong—three women who later became Mary's "faithful friends" and who were immensely helpful in furthering Bryan's career. Differences were not limited to these two societies; in fact, disagreements escalated within the Penwith circle the following year when attempts were made to categorize abstract and representational artists into "A" and "B" groups.

Peter Lanyon was one of the younger artists caught up in this tribal-artistic warfare of West Cornwall. Exasperated by the factionalism of the St. Ives scene, he transferred his enormous energy and enthusiasm to Newlyn and advocated that the long-established Newlyn Art Gallery, founded in 1895, accept contemporary artists working in an eclectic range of styles—a move which would lead to Bryan's first one-man exhibition in 1959.

Much of the Penwith discontent abated when the "A" and "B" controversy was dropped and the society's gallery at 18 Fore Street was vacated in favor of a smaller one nearby. This move led the Penwith Society to find a larger permanent location four years later. A close friend of both Ben Nicholson and Barbara Hepworth, Sir Herbert Read, the respected critic and poet, was appointed president of the Penwith group and he opened the new gallery in July 1957. Three months later Bryan exhibited his work there for the first time as an associate member.

The theories of physician Christopher Woodard interested Mary, and after reading several of his works on the power of faith and the remarkable recoveries made outside the conventional procedures of medicine she wrote to him explaining her plight.

"He answered immediately," Mary recalled, "and said that he knew I was meant to contact him because he was soon coming to Cornwall to visit for the first time in his life." Mary never forgot the way Dr. Woodard "bounded" up the stairs of their home above the butcher shop at Market Place and how his presence brought a glow of optimism.

His first words upon entering her living room were "It doesn't seem possible that you have two children as you say you do—I sense such a wonderful feeling in this home."

"Little was known about phenylketonuria at that time," said Mary—the year was 1958, "and it was just as if he saw the handwriting on the wall. He said to me: 'Before I see your children, I want to tell you that diet plays a tremendous factor in their lives.' "

The two talked at length of the difficulties involved in keeping alive a semblance of normalcy under such conditions, and then Mary called the children in to meet him. Margaretta charmed Dr. Woodard with her "happy-go-lucky smile," and typically, the son shyly shook hands and politely greeted the visitor.

Dr. Woodard's opinion of Bryan remained steadfast over the years. "I thought of him and his life as the pathway to genius," he wrote decades later, "and prayed that it might be fulfilled as such, for I had always thought of genius as the greatest manifestation of Almighty God's creative energy."

Bryan had at this time completed his first few oils, and since one of Dr. Woodard's many activities was painting he immediately wanted to see them. Mary was grateful for his interest but had some apprehension. "I brought them out," she recalled, "and he said they were lovely. Then he placed his hands on Bryan's head and said: 'Now Bryan, I'm going to pray to God for nothing less than genius as far as your paintings are concerned.' " For Mary, these few words seemed to be a turning point in her son's life—a straightening of the road ahead. After this first meeting and blessing, she noticed an increase of confidence, and more stability in his work habits.

The church has been a special place for Bryan since childhood, and many of his paintings, both interior and exterior views, reveal the central role it plays in his life. Stone on stone it rises, and when he passes this edifice there is fervor and respect in his voice as he says aloud, "St. Ives Church. St. Ia Church." There were occasions when Mary felt her son attended services too diligently—more than two Sunday appearances attracted comments. "For a few weeks," she told me, "he only went twice, but I soon had to remind him again."

Walter, a staunch Methodist, attended Sunday evening services, and Bryan accompanied his father. The two sat in their usual place up front, and when the service began, Bryan was quick to rise and sing the opening hymn robustly. This was the one place where he felt at ease—enough so that he could turn and smile at familiar faces and friends.

Margaretta, in her own way, enjoyed the music as much as her brother did, though she was unable to concentrate for long periods as her attention wandered. Mary, uncomfortably aware that her daughter was disturbing those who sat nearby, hustled her from the church, and at times these departures occurred before the sermon got underway. It was easier and less nerve-racking to stay at home and await Bryan's full and enthusiastic report of what went on, the hymns selected, and who sang the best in full voice.

Sunday morning services were more relaxing. She and Margaretta left Walter and Bryan by the door and entered the adjoining Lady Chapel. Here the two could sit unseen by most of the parishioners, join in the singing—the girl cooing in tune—and listen to the service. If her daughter had a bad case of the jitters, they could slip out the side door without being disruptive. Mary, who allowed her life to be steered by her children's needs and wishes, couldn't resist when she felt Margaretta tugging at her dress impatiently as they prepared for church. That eager smile when the church bells began ringing moved Mary deeply.

There were many things in the Lady Chapel to engage Margaretta's attention: she could watch the boys in the choir; gaze at the colorful tapestries and ornate carvings; and admire a recent Barbara Hepworth sculpture of the Madonna and Child, done in white marble, and donated by Hepworth in memory of her son, Paul, who had died in a Thailand airplane accident. Bryan and her father could be seen when she looked back into the nave of the church, and the way her brother sang hymns amused Margaretta.

* * *

Mary also exhibited at Bryan's second Penwith Gallery showing in 1958, and both received favorable notice: "Mr Pearce has a natural instinct for colour and often uses thick, sweet pinks in combination with a pungent acid green and a dash of orange," wrote the reviewer, and then observed, "Mary Pearce has used the charm of strange pinks to make her Christmas roses glow." This brief comment on her work pleased Mary, but what was written about Bryan was more important.

Mother and son painting in adjoining rooftop studios above a butcher shop was newsworthy enough to send a reporter hustling to Market Place. Mary, with her instinctive flair for publicity, lost no time in revealing that Bryan was preparing work for two 1959 exhibitions—his first one-man show at the Newlyn Gallery near Penzance, and a three-man show with Guy Worsdell and Shearer Armstrong at The Scottish Gallery in Edinburgh. There were several press notices of these two events and one reporter concluded with "Bryan Pearce is a young painter, and it will be interesting to watch his development."

"Sometimes, when we were alone in the evening, my husband and I would get talking about Bryan's success as a painter," said Mary, "and it just seemed impossible that this could be happening to him. There were so many years when he didn't have any kind of a future, and we had to live from day to day. For us, it was a miracle."

Paintings meant little to Margaretta, and the unexpected attention her brother was getting didn't arouse jealousy. She was amused to see one of Bryan's harbor scenes on display in the Fore Street Gallery where the Penwith Society was holding their annual exhibit. Margaretta tugged at Audrey's arm and motioned her surprise at seeing a familiar object in a different place, then quickly lost interest.

That first one-man show is a red-letter occasion in an artist's life, and most painters look upon this day with apprehension. Bryan was untouched by it all as he watched his mother prepare invitation cards for the private view at the Newlyn Gallery on Saturday, April 29, 1959.

Mary was the one who agonized as the crucial date neared. She was sensitive to public opinion and sometimes worried that her son's childlike pictures might be misunderstood or disparaged by sophisticated viewers. Even more troubling was the thought of Bryan being the center of attention. Would he stand "stiff as a poker" at her side or would he mutter some "silly nonsense" when friendly strangers approached him?

The Pearces lingered by the entrance as friends and local artists came for the private viewing: Walter's benign countenance kept his concerns hidden, Mary nervously clutched her son's arm, and a smiling Bryan greeted each guest politely in the same tone of voice. The room soon filled, and Mary began to relax as she mingled and overheard a number of laudatory comments. The pictures were well lighted and spaced appealingly along the walls, and there were several buyers.

Bryan, unaware of his success, toured the gallery and approached each painting shyly for a closer look. When an effusive comment was hurled in his direction, he nodded with dignity, looked pleased, and didn't rush off as Mary had feared. For him, the best moment of the entire afternoon came when his father stood beside him and said, "Your paintings look very well, Bryan."

Margaretta was waiting on the window seat overlooking the street when her parents and Bryan returned home triumphantly that day. Audrey was delighted that all had gone well, and Margaretta was happy because everyone was happy—it was impossible to explain to this grown child the significance of her brother's success. "I used to think she missed so much in life," said Mary, "but I always felt less troubled when I saw her face light up."

From her window seat in the first-floor living room, Margaretta had a panoramic view of life: there were bustling winter shoppers and strolling summer visitors; across the street by the church door, she saw people gather for christenings, weddings, funerals; and in the distance there were boats entering and leaving the harbor. "I often wondered what went on in her mind while she sat there," said Mary. "She seemed so contented and cheerful."

Margaretta frequently wandered up the stairs to the studios. Bryan ignored her as he sat hunched at his easel—he now was ensconced in a well-planned routine that Mary had structured for him. There were no complications or interruptions worth bothering with while he unemotionally filled with paint the shapes he had outlined.

Mary safeguarded her son's privacy as much as she could, made sure there were suitable supplies of paints and canvases, and saw to the framing. When the promotion of his work vastly increased her correspondence, she enrolled in a typewriting class in Penzance. Margaretta enjoyed watching her mother's busy fingers at the keyboard, but soon the young woman's attention strayed and she was back at the window seat.

She loved being with her male cousins and could be quite flirtatious with her beckoning eyes and secret smiles. "How different her life would have been," said Mary, "if the cure for phenylketonuria had been discovered earlier—she missed it by only a few years."

Walter's mother at Eden House was losing her hearing, and when she spoke her voice had a strange sort of cadence. Margaretta found Granny Pearce's unusual pattern of speech hilarious and often would break into uncontrollable laughter—even Mrs. Pearce was amused and joined in the merriment. In this family, there was no need to commiserate over physical shortcomings.

There were highlights in Margaretta's day: she enjoyed her walks with Audrey along the harbor and up the footpath to Carbis Bay when she called on her Warmington grandparents; at home, there were loving parents, records to play, games with Audrey, and her window seat to the world.

Only Mary was awake and burdened with sentry duty as midnight thoughts crowded the barricades of hope. She knew, while turning in her half sleep, that the fits had their own spasmodic schedule. They kept coming, darkly dependable and relentless: she would get up, straighten the tangled bedclothes, and smooth her daughter's brow—somehow, Margaretta slept through these seizures. At last, when noises in the street below returned, Mary drew open the curtains in the girl's room and was thankful to find her still alive.

It was obvious to Mary that her daughter was soothed by the atmosphere of the church and loved being there. Sometimes, on weekdays, the girl would grasp her mother's hand and lead her into the empty chapel so they could pray together. Margaretta seemed more trusting than Bryan in accepting the love of God. His interests lay in the singing of hymns and learning more of the simple prayers and responses.

Aware that religion was becoming an increasingly important part of their lives, Mary was convinced that their faith would be strengthened if her two children received communion. When the parish priest next visited her, she brought up the prospect of confirmation. To her dismay, he displayed little enthusiasm. Margaretta's speech handicap and inability to follow instructions made it impossible for her to be accepted at the communion table; Bryan, perhaps in time, would be ready—but only after long application and suitable preparation.

"I was very hurt," said Mary, "and I had no intention of going ahead with confirmation plans." She felt her daughter's innocence and goodness were more meaningful in the eyes of God than any formality performed to achieve a state of grace.

Margaretta at 18½ years

Word of his parish priest's decision soon reached the Bishop of Truro, and as a gesture he visited Mary. Margaretta greeted him in her usual charming manner, and the embarrassed bishop did his best to offer guidance. It was a dilemma of some consequence, he told Mary, and the problem needed more time and deliberation. Before the uncomfortable prelate took leave, he spoke gently to Margaretta and promised to visit her again in a few months—this meeting took place only a few weeks before her death.

"Margaretta's attacks would always come at night," said Mary. "So this meant that I didn't have a good night's rest for ten years. I would listen for these attacks, and I knew her death would happen. I realized that sometime I wouldn't hear her, and I *didn't* hear her one night. I found her in the morning. She had fallen over the bed and had been suffocated. She was nineteen and a half. We knew just a year before she died she had phenylketonuria."

"What causes phenylketonuria?" I asked Mary.

"A doctor told me it was the kind of thing that gets handed down like duodenal ulcers, and I have heard it has something to do with the metabolism."

(Since the time of this conversation in 1968, considerable research has been done on the causes of phenylketonuria [PKU]. Treatment has been available only since the late 1950s, and doctors, biochemists, and dietitians are still learning about PKU, particularly how it is inherited and what is effective in the treatment of adults.)

"Now every baby is tested at birth," said Mary, "and if they are found to have the disease, they are put on a special diet immediately."

The foods we consume contain protein, one part of which (phenylalanine) cannot be broken down by the person with PKU. Without treatment this leads to impaired brain development, and a controlled diet can prevent such deterioration. There are a number of foods not permitted in a phenylalanine diet, such as poultry, fish, meat, eggs, cheese, and bread and cakes made with ordinary flour.

"All the children with phenylketonuria," Mary told me, "have blond hair and are very fair. But once they are given the special diet their hair becomes dark. Children with this disease are born with perfect brains which begin to deteriorate at the age of six months."

"When does this deterioration stop?"

"Researchers don't know yet—they've only had young children to study. I remember a doctor who came to one of Bryan's shows in London, and he was so terribly interested because he had never seen an adult with the disease. This doctor arrived at the show around six in the evening and stayed until we left at nine. He said to me after looking at the paintings and watching Bryan for the longest time, 'Mrs. Pearce, we are witnessing a miracle. I can't believe your son has accomplished so much!' A mental health specialist, a woman who examines Bryan regularly, told me that they don't know whether the acid is still doing damage by the time a person reaches maturity. But having known Bryan for seven years and seeing what a fantastic change there has been in him, she feels that it is possible that the acid has done its worst."

"Acid?"

"Amino acid. A portion of the digestive organ doesn't secrete a particular chemical, and through the lack of that chemical, an acid is set up. It's this which damages certain cells of the brain."

(What is currently accepted is that a strict low phenylalanine diet must be maintained during the developing years, and the present evidence suggests that limited diet restrictions should continue throughout life. Some adults with PKU have nervous system disorders, such as hand tremors or poor coordination. Many adult sufferers find they can concentrate better when their blood levels of phenylalanine are within the normal range.)

Mary remembered the day when the mental health advisor who visited routinely to check on the well-being of Bryan and Margaretta delivered news that was of particular interest. It now had been established that an ordinary diet—nourishing foods such as milk and eggs—damaged the central nervous system of children born with a certain kind of metabolic deficiency. Dr. Woodard's prophetic diagnosis that diet played a crucial part in her children's disability had now been confirmed.

(PKU is inherited as an autosomal recessive disorder. Each parent must carry one defective gene in order for there to be the risk that an infant will have PKU. Under these circumstances, there is a one in four possibility that the baby will have phenylketonuria. It is estimated that one in every 15,000 newborns is stricken with PKU in the United States, and the incidences vary in other parts of the world.)

"Why should this happen to us?" Mary asked her family doctor, and she was told that the fault was in the genes. Somewhere in the long and healthy ancestry of the Warmington and Pearce families there was a genetic disorder. "Why *two* children?" she asked, but the question went unanswered.

Walter and Mary often took Bryan to the country churches around West Cornwall and waited in the pews while he drew for future paintings. If some elaborate mosaic of floor tile or carving on a prayer bench trapped his attention, he would devote much of his time penciling the pattern faintly but carefully into his sketchbook. Mary frequently worried that he would lose perspective. She learned eventually that it made little difference; Bryan included everything he felt to be essential, whether it was done on location or when he returned home.

Painters usually develop their techniques slowly, frequently stumbling before mastering their craft. Bryan established his methods early, thus eliminating many of the problems confronting most professionals. He also became increasingly decisive in his selection of things to paint and in the way he would interpret them: hills became smooth hummocks of color, roads were gray ribbons centered by broad white traffic lines, and vegetation was reduced to a leaf motif. Gulls rarely circled his harbor scenes, there were never storm clouds or shadows, and only occasionally did he include animals or people. Mary was tempted at times to draw attention to some new object. "Oh look, Bryan," she would say, "wouldn't that be nice to include!" He would give whatever his mother suggested a perfunctory glance and would reply, "I don't want to paint it."

I said to Mary: "Bryan has a painting of Christ being taken down from the Cross, but in the picture there is no Christ. Do you have an explanation for this?"

And her answer: "I have no idea. This sort of thing you will find in much of his work. He leaves out things that are the most obvious. If there is something out of sight, or behind him, and if he wants it for his composition, he'll put it in. Now he did one from our lounge window. Outside, there is a plain gray road. In his painting he put tiny telephone hatches in the middle of it. I suppose the road was too plain for him, and he wanted something additional."

An omission, similar to the absent Christ being taken down from the Cross, occurred in a later painting of several figures playing ball on the beach. For some mysterious reason, perhaps for the sake of composition or a sudden decision that the ball was of little consequence, Bryan omitted it. Mary knew there was little point in asking him why he did such things; the last time she questioned him about this he simply replied, "That's how I like it."

"Do *you* have any idea what motivates him to include or exclude things in his paintings?" I asked Mary.

"No," she replied. "I remember we were passing Land's End airport one afternoon, and since there were a lot of people around we stopped to see what was happening. It proved to be opening day at the heliport and there was a helicopter. When we got home Bryan said he thought he would draw the airport, and when I saw his drawing I found hills and trees. I asked why he drew these—there is only sea and sky in that area. He said, 'I had to put something there.' "

Several weeks later, Bryan wanted to watch another helicopter take off and land. This request surprised his parents because he had shown so little interest while they were at the airport.

"I rang up the heliport in Penzance," recalled Mary, "to find out what time the helicopter would be in so Bryan could draw it. Walter and I drove over with Misomé Peile and her mother. After we had been there for a while, Misomé asked me if I had seen what Bryan was doing. He was drawing a fence while the helicopter was landing. I told him he could do that later, but he kept at this barricade that was crisscrossed with wire. We had given up an entire morning to take him there, and all he had done was just the fence. But at home that afternoon he drew all the trains in the background and the helicopter. He did them all from memory."

As Bryan's work progressed, the colors became clearer and the lines more definite; grays and deep browns he had used in earlier paintings were now fresher, and a brighter light warmed his buildings, harbors, and hills. The accuracy of his memory in rendering details amazed admirers who knew his limitations. Years after *The Scillonian*, a passenger ship, had docked at St. Ives, he was able to recall the exact placement of her cranes, funnel, masts, and portholes.

"How does Bryan react to criticism?"

"I don't think he minds," said Mary. "Years ago, before I realized he shouldn't be told things about his paintings, I would tell him that some things were not right in a picture, and he would ask if he had spoiled it. I don't criticize or make him alter a thing now. But if I should say, 'I didn't think it looked like that,' or 'Where did you get that idea from?' he will say, 'I'm quite happy with it.' I sometimes say, 'I don't like this picture as much as the other one.' His reply is always, 'Some people like one thing and some people like another. I'm quite happy with it.' "

"Is he pleased," I asked, "when people say they like his paintings?"

"It encourages him," Mary replied. "But I think the greatest thing of all is that *we* are pleased. At his last show in London he came up to me and said, 'There are some red stars on my pictures. That means they have been sold. Are you proud of me?' "

Bryan got the elementary technique of painting from his mother, and certainly her flair for color helped to solidify his choices, particularly in the early still lifes and St. Ives townscapes. Once the suggestions were habituated through repetition, he was able to make his own decisions, and she had the instinctive good sense not to interfere. It would have been so easy for Mary to say: "No Bryan, things aren't done that way!" Instead, she wisely stepped back and allowed him his own creative space. This was when she quickly and ably assumed the roles of secretary, archivist, and promoter.

"Did he learn how to mix colors at Mr. Fuller's?" I asked.

"I don't know how much Mr. Fuller taught him about that," she replied. "I think Bryan always has been able to mix colors. He never asks how to get a particular shade, and he never uses a color straight from the tube. He always puts the smallest touch of something else with it. I sometimes see him just showing a brush with one color on it—showing it to another. You should see how gently he does it. It's lovely to watch him mix his paints. Just a touch here and a touch there. He does it with such love."

"Has there been any noticeable change in his palette since he started working in oils?"

"I think his colors have become brighter, though he can paint some things in subtle shades. I remember a still life he just recently sold. It had so much color you could just put your arms around it!"

"Is he able to *recall* how he got a particular shade?"

"Oh yes. I remember a picture which came back from Toronto in need of repair. He only has one layer of paint on his canvases, and this picture had been scratched. I was touching it up for him. I said, 'I have never seen you do a road with this color, Bryan. It's neither gray nor brown. I don't know what it is.' He glanced at it and said, 'A bit of black, a bit of white, and a touch of orange.' When I put the touch of orange in it, the shade was just right. But if someone told him how to mix a color, he wouldn't remember it."

"His studio is so neatly arranged and clean," I remarked. "Is this your doing?"

Mary looked surprised.

"Oh no!" she said. "He has always been tidy. I remember a Catholic priest—he was one of Mr. Fuller's students—told me that Bryan taught him a lesson that he would never forget. Bryan came up to him during one of the little intervals of rest, stared at the priest's brushes and said, 'Look at your dirty brushes!' Bryan wouldn't dream of going to bed at night without cleaning and tidying everything. He takes great care of his painting equipment—it means so much to him."

"I should think some of his more complicated landscapes would be very difficult to do—particularly those with so many houses and done with a perspective that reminded Mr. Fuller of a 'map.' "

"The only time he has trouble now is when he doesn't get his first drawing right. But that doesn't happen very often. I remember he had difficulty with one of his pictures of the interior of our church. A gentleman here in St. Ives who paints—he's not really an artist—went into the church and saw him drawing. He said to Bryan, 'You have your window too high up.' That put Bryan off. When I went to the church to tell him that lunch was ready, he said, 'I couldn't draw the window over the altar. I had it too high and then a man came and told me that I had it too high and when I put it down lower it still wasn't right.' Bryan has never forgotten that picture."

One evening Mary had a conversation with an artist whose paintings were crowded with figures. He explained that he was a lonely man and painted people for company. The idea intrigued but worried Mary: her son's pictures rarely had humans; his scenes were deserted streets and lonesome hillsides.

"You must not be troubled by that," he told her.

"Don't you find it a bit unusual?" she asked.

"Not at all," he said. "And you should be glad that his streets *are* deserted."

"Why?"

"Because Mrs. Pearce," the man replied, "Bryan is not a lonely person—he doesn't need people in his paintings the way I do."

Bryan missed seeing his sister but showed no signs of being downcast. "Our Margaretta," he told his mother, "is up in Heaven with Jesus." He calmly accepted her absence as if she had gone to see Granny Pearce or to visit some relative in Carbis Bay.

Her daughter's death nearly overwhelmed Mary, and she sometimes blamed herself for being asleep that fateful night. With Margaretta gone and no longer needing her help, Audrey found work elsewhere in town. Market Place seemed strangely quiet and empty now, and Mary realized that she must keep busy. She did have time to paint in her studio but preferred to be with people and to accomplish what she could in promoting Bryan's work.

She found excitement in making new contacts with the art world and dealing with professionals. By studying the art magazines carefully, she learned the formalities required for the submission of paintings to various galleries. Bryan's associate membership with the Penwith Society was fortunate as this allowed him to exhibit with leading painters from the area. Mary now was convinced that her son's originality deserved increased exposure.

There were, however, several St. Ives friends and acquaintances who looked upon Bryan's paintings as objects of a failed therapy: they couldn't get past the clinical aspects of his childhood and had little faith in the early watercolors. In the mind's eye of their mind-set, they still saw a tormented child teetering dangerously at the edge of a pier while shouting at trains.

The 1961 Annual Show Day—when visitors are invited to the studios—attracted attention to Bryan's paintings. Mary was surprised and delighted with the coverage given by *The St. Ives Times and Echo* on April 13, 1961:

"In spite of rain and mist hundreds of visitors poured into St. Ives on Easter Monday for the Annual Show Day. This picturesque event had its origin in the days when there were no galleries—now the town has four. Bryan Pearce's breathtakingly colourful Exhibition in the 'Roof Top Studio' showed that he had approached the most awe-inspiring problems of composition with incredible confidence and assurance."

Bryan's second one-man show took place during the summer of 1961 at the Sail Loft Gallery in St. Ives. This small but active establishment had been founded by Lithuanian-born artist Elena Gaputyte, who promoted the work of new talents. The gallery was simply arranged and had an informal atmosphere—an ideal place for paintings by Bryan Pearce.

Some residents of St. Ives had been watching his progress and hadn't forgotten that during the nineteen thirties another hometown original, Alfred Wallis, had been dismissed as a peculiar crank who painted crazily on cardboard. Twenty years later, Wallis's reputation was worldwide, and the recipients of his pictures—those who had thrown away his painted jugs and uneven scraps of cardboard—were strangely quiet.

Bryan's work soon received attention from the London magazine *Freedom*. Reviewer Arthur Moyse interviewed Mary and recorded his impressions. "There is a silence in the studio his mother has made for him at the top of the house that they have named *Chylowen* (the house of love)," wrote Moyse. "Bryan Pearce lives within his shuttered world and works without models, without aid and without advice...the sweetness of his soul has illuminated the dark corners of his mind."

Arthur Moyse's piece in *Freedom* helped to circulate word of Bryan's originality. This came at a time when London artists were analyzing the intellectual content of their work. Keith Colquhoun wrote the catalog introduction to Bryan's one-man show at London's St. Martin's Gallery in 1962 and described the paintings as coming from a "seductive world of seemingly scented seas and sugar-coated houses inhabited by people living through an endless succession of birthdays!" To draw attention to this dreamland, one of Bryan's "all round" harbor scenes was displayed on the catalog. The well-circulated *Arts Review* noted with approval that there seemed to be a "total abandonment of perspective" in many of the paintings.

Suddenly, Mary was besieged with offers to exhibit her son's work outside the country, and she quickly sent paintings for the UNESCO Exhibition in Monte Carlo, to a Spotorno, Italy gallery, and to the Minotaur Gallery in Toronto, Canada.

When Mary tried to explain how important it was to have his paintings exhibited in faraway countries, Bryan stared at her with no sign of comprehension. She got out a map of the world and showed him where Canada, Monaco, and Italy were located. He politely followed her finger as she pinpointed them; she could see it was impossible for him to imagine what went on in these strange places. The significance of being recognized in the art world eluded him, though he did understand what it meant when red stars were placed by his paintings at shows. "They've been sold," he proudly told his mother. "Now I can pay my bills."

In 1962, the BBC asked Mary and Walter if they would grant permission for a television feature on Bryan. The film would cover his daily life, his painting, and there would be a sensitive coverage of Bryan's disability and achievements. The Pearces had some misgivings but realized that this was an opportunity for furthering their son's career. Upon receiving an outline of the script and consulting with friends, they accepted the proposal. Cornish poet Charles Causley arrived in St. Ives to discuss the project, and Mary liked him immediately.

Then came the camera crew with their cables and growling lenses. It would be a "*simple* script" a technician briskly informed the Pearces, just "an ordinary day" with their son quietly following his usual activities.

When everything was in place and the filming about to begin, a proud Bryan appeared dressed in one of his finest suits. He politely greeted them all and was eager to do his best. Mary had spent time coaching him on how to behave, but in such an alien gathering she was unable to suppress the notion that a fiasco was in the making.

The first order of business would be to follow young Pearce on his usual morning walk down the narrow cobbled street and along the harborside walkway to West Pier. At the inception of this drama, the artist must be seen exiting his house by Wills Lane; a bit of local color would be added with a shot of him passing The Golden Lion tavern, and then a slow take when he crossed the road to the harbor. "Now Bryan," an anxious Mary told him before he set out, "please remember! All I ask is that you keep your head up." He still had a tendency to hold his head sideways at an awkward angle.

Bryan emerged from the doorway with chin up and seemingly oblivious of the hubbub around him. He began to march proudly across the road and after several steps he was stopped and asked to repeat the performance. He obligingly returned, but this time seemed more wooden as he stepped into the street. Mary stood near the window, out of sight, watching this staged rehearsal with increased misgivings. He was called back to the doorway again, and now the instructions were less kind. Mary immediately understood the dilemma: for years, she and Walter had impressed on him the importance of walking by the side of the road away from traffic, and here were these strangers telling him to ignore this long-standing advice. "I was tempted to go out and speak to Bryan," she recalled, "but I didn't want to intrude or add to the confusion."

Finally, the exasperated director solved the problem by having one of his crew chalk a line along the center of the road, and after some coaxing Bryan reluctantly agreed to break training and jaywalk his way to the harbor.

Mary hurried up the stairs to the studio, and from the high window she was able to watch her son lead his bizarre band of followers along the pier. At this point, another batch of incomprehensible orders was issued while Bryan sat awkwardly on a granite mooring post and stared at a frantic director who was gesturing wildly. From a distance, the man's theatrical movements were comical enough for Mary to suppress a giggle, though she did feel regret for causing her son to be subjected to such turmoil. When the director's frustration peaked, Bryan was asked to give up his seat in order for this film professional to demonstrate how a promising young artist should conduct himself in hometown surroundings.

Mary knew there would be a confrontation, and it came as soon as the camera crew and Bryan returned to the house. The unhappy director insisted that she speak to him alone. As they went into the kitchen Mary was prepared to be helpful and sympathetic. "Mrs. Pearce," he began without preliminaries, "I am getting no cooperation from your son, and I find he is quite impossible to film." The way he said it aroused her anger—she thought the man rude and insensitive. "You were not asked to come," she told him and allowed her reply to fade into an uncomfortable silence.

A time-out was declared while the camera crew recovered and Mary calmed an anxious and puzzled Bryan. Perhaps a simple domestic shot would relieve nervous tension, the filmmakers decided—some morning routine easy to execute. A few frames showing the painter making his bed might fit snugly into the sequence. Immediately, preparations began for the filming, and Bryan watched with concern while his radio, a prized possession, was hustled from the shelf by the bed and placed in another location.

A cameraman had pulled back a corner of the bedclothes, and Bryan was expected to smooth the pillow and tuck in the turned cover—just two quick motions. But what they requested did not relate to his many years of training; his mother had instilled in him that every household chore should be done thoroughly, and the clumsy man had loosened all the blankets and sheets. Bryan stripped the bed, and a commotion of flapping bedclothes in the small chamber further delayed the filming while he conscientiously completed the task.

These out-of-context duties before a camera bewildered him, and the testiness of the director caused him to look anxiously at his mother for some explanation as to what he was doing wrong. She tried to console him, but there were subtleties at work here beyond his comprehension. The ordeal went on into a second day before all the celluloid pantomimes of their son's uncomplicated life had been performed. Mary and Walter were delighted to have the crew gone but wondered nervously how many of the blunders and tense moments would be seen by thousands of viewers when the film was run.

A month or two later, Mary invited a number of friends and relations, along with Leonard Fuller and his wife, to watch the premiere of this BBC production. To his parents' astonishment, all of Bryan's ungainly movements and robotlike responses seemed to dissolve in a heightened depiction of his unusual life and personality. Bryan viewed the scenes with some interest and renewed alarm, and after being congratulated by everyone present he retreated to his room at the head of the stairs and began to play records.

In open competition with two thousand five hundred submissions, Bryan's oil *Portreath No. 2*, 1961, was selected for the 1963-1964 prestigious Fourth John Moores Exhibition at the Walker Art Gallery in Liverpool. His paintings were now being displayed alongside work by leading contemporary British artists.

Critics were undecided when estimating his affinities to other painters and tracking his sources of influence. Some reviewers commented on the "naïveté" and "innocent vision" of his compositions; the detailed St. Ives townscapes brought to mind the French primitive painter Louis Vivin. Braque and Matisse were also mentioned when his still lifes and interiors were discussed.

Journalist Ian Mayes was so impressed with one of Bryan's paintings on display at the Penwith Gallery that he, together with his wife and young daughter, called on the Pearces at their Market Place home in 1963. Mary greeted them, and in a January 22, 2000 letter to Janet Axten, Mayes recalled that they all "seemed to become friends quite quickly"—Bryan even took Ian on an evening walk around St. Ives.

Mayes submitted a feature on Bryan to *The Guardian* under the title "The Miracle Painter of St Ives." The article was illustrated with a photograph of the artist at his easel working on *Penzance Harbour All Round*, 1963, and there was a reproduction of his clothesline painting *Monday*, 1959. Instead of appearing in the art section of the newspaper, Mayes's piece was published on January 17, 1964 in a popular column reserved for editor Mary Stott where it received greater attention.

The account of how "the thirty-four year old son of a retired butcher" found recognition as an authentic primitive artist also revealed details of his early brain damage. "These are facts which, until now," wrote Mayes, "when Pearce can fairly be said to have something of a reputation as an artist have been deliberately concealed. Pearce's mother, Mrs Mary Pearce and admirers of his paintings, wisely decided that his work should stand or fall purely on its artistic merits. Any biographical notes, for this reason, have always been omitted from Pearce exhibition programmes."

There was a new "equanimity and sense of peace" in Bryan's paintings, and Mayes remembered the words written about an anonymous Chinese artist which Mary had hung up in her son's studio: "His life and his work are full of the miracle of simple things and his heart is at peace."

Mayes also told his readers that Bryan's creations promised future sales. "For four years now his paintings have paid for his clothes and the cost of his paints." These contributions to the family budget coincided with Walter's 1963 retirement after nearly fifty years of work in the butcher shop. It amazed both Walter and Mary that their son was achieving some financial independence.

He was painting some of his best townscapes at this time—they were pictures with considerable detail and not work that could be hurried. It made no difference to him what arrangements his mother finalized for displaying his work; he painted carefully and at the same steady pace.

There was additional publicity in 1964 when Taurus Artists of London published George T. Noszlopy's monograph *The Primitive Art of Bryan Pearce*. Noszlopy, a freelance essayist and an art history lecturer at the City of Coventry College of Art, visited the Pearces several times while preparing his study.

The booklet, containing 5 pages of text and 21 black-and-white illustrations of Bryan's watercolors and oils from 1952 to 1963, had this conclusion: "The story of Bryan Pearce's paintings is the history of a painter created by his art rather than the history of an artistic style created by its painter. This makes his pictures unique. This simple unity of his works appeals to our aesthetic needs and this makes them part of modern Western art." Noszlopy believed that Bryan's medical history formatted the artist's creations since it was "an emotional response rather than an intellectual attitude by which he is able to give a unified form to fragmentary reality."

Mary gave me a copy of Noszlopy's study, and when discussing it with her I detected both the immense pride she took in the publication and her bewilderment when deciphering its contents.

"It is certainly wonderful for Bryan," she told me.

"I think your help for young Bryan Pearce has been excellent," Peter Lanyon wrote Leonard Fuller. "It is cheering to think that his life has

Bryan Pearce, early 1960s

been transformed by his Art." Lanyon, a St. Ives native and well-known painter, had recommended Bryan's work to the membership while serving as chairman for the Newlyn Society of Artists. This led to Bryan's first one-man show at their gallery in 1959. Mary, aware of Peter Lanyon's reputation and somewhat intimidated, finally wrote asking him if he would contribute a short catalog introduction for her son's second one-man exhibition at the St. Martin's Gallery. He replied almost immediately with the suggested text. "I have tried to keep it simple and direct and I hope you will not object to my attempt to place Bryan in the St Ives Art Scene. I think this is a thing I can do, as a native, and at the same time warn about the dangers which lie waiting for many of our artists."

The harbour, the coastguard or the bridge over the railway happen to Bryan Pearce who is a native of St Ives. All these things have an activity which is not only seen, there is evidence in every painting of an awareness which is more direct, the knowing which a man will have for land or sea or craft. When this understanding is linked to the kind of play which is common in child art, the combination is called Folk Art. If a category is necessary, Bryan Pearce is nearest to this.

His art emerges at a time when sophistication is disintegrating St Ives painting, and a self-conscious group of artists is mourning the decline of a fictitious 'St Ives School.' Bryan Pearce takes a walk to Carbis Bay, returning by the cliff path to paint what has happened with a blue sea and green grass and side-seen houses and around-corner looks, that have been avoided in the quaint and pretty concept of picture postcard St Ives, and exploited in boutique primitivism. Because his sources are not seen with a passive eye, but are truly happenings, his painting is original.

Theory and speculation usually put distance between the event and its description, and the painting is subjected to stretching by miles of elastic words, so that the acts of observing, making and communicating are all studied out of context. These paintings may be subjects for analysis to some people but that activity is not going to make the paintings more understandable. It is necessary to accept these works as the labour of a man who has to communicate this way because there is no other. It is then possible to celebrate the facts and not the theory.

The director of the St. Martin's Gallery hoped that Mary, Walter and Bryan would attend the private view in London before the exhibit's May 18th opening, but the thought of going frightened Mary. Private views at local galleries with friends and sympathetic acquaintances were intimidating enough, and she could envision the horror of mingling with total strangers and sophisticated critics from the London art world. How would Bryan respond in such a gathering?

Mary and Walter Pearce, 1962

"What are we ever going to do?" Mary asked Barbara Hepworth.

"Well," replied Hepworth, "Picasso doesn't go to his own private views."

The problem was solved when Bryan had one of his occasional attacks of tracheitis, brought about by long walks in windy weather. A relieved Mary telegraphed her regrets and medicated her son. In spite of their absence, the show was hugely successful and the paintings were well received.

Studio International later reprinted the text of Lanyon's introduction. His perceptive assessment was made more poignant by a tragic event which occurred shortly after the piece was written: Peter Lanyon died in a glider accident.

The reception given Bryan's work at the 1964 St. Martin's Gallery exhibition made Mary feel more at home in the art world. She soon became less apprehensive about attending private views, and now that Bryan had gained acceptance through his paintings, her earlier frustration at his being considered an outsider had diminished considerably. She was confident that her son could look as suave as any metropolitan in the new suit and tie he had so carefully chosen for himself.

Bryan's paintings were beginning to be acquired for private and public collections, and his individual style was instantly recognizable in British museums and galleries. There was a launching parallel: just as the art of Alfred Wallis had been revealed by Ben Nicholson and Christopher Wood, Bryan's work had been purchased by Barbara Hepworth and several other well-known artists.

When Mary held a small exhibit of her son's paintings at Market Place, she sold two oils and three watercolors to a Mr. H. S. Ede. The stranger explained that he didn't have any money with him and had forgotten his checkbook. Would she trust him? Mary appreciated his interest and decided to take a chance. She had no knowledge of Jim Ede's reputation: that he had been affiliated with the Tate Gallery in London and was to present his large collection of Alfred Wallis paintings along with other contemporary works to the University of Cambridge.

Another admirer who came to Market Place when Mary was exhibiting Bryan's work in aid of the local hospital was Alan Bowness. This was the beginning of a long and invaluable friendship. He was then a lecturer at the Courtauld Institute, a member of the Art Council, and a leading authority on twentieth century painting. (In her last letter to me, September 16, 1996, Mary wrote: "Whenever I am uncertain, I ask the advice of my friend Sir Alan Bowness & I always rely on his judgement.") When Bryan had his first one-man show at the New Art Centre in London in 1966, Bowness agreed to write the catalog introduction.

These enchanting sunlit paintings are mostly of St Ives—the boats in the harbour, the fishermen's cottages and gardens, the parish church that one sees below Bryan Pearce's studio window. It is a serene untroubled world that reflects the natural innocence and delight of a man who has found relief and rehabilitation through painting. For Bryan Pearce has suffered since childhood from a crippling mental illness (phenylketonuria) that has made normal communication impossible for him, and in Peter Lanyon's words he '...has to communicate this way because there is no other.'

More remarkable than a beneficial therapeutic effect, however, has been the growth and emergence of an artist. Practice has brought with it a certain professionalism and the formal qualities, the feeling for space and colour and composition in these works, are often striking. The originality of vision remains unchanged and unspoilt because in the circumstances nothing else is possible, nor can there be any conscious 'influences', for precisely the same reason.

It is a most unusual combination closer to what Dubuffet calls *L'art brut* than to naïve painting or child art. It could happen only in a place like St Ives (think of Alfred Wallis), and the particular homage to his native Cornwall that Bryan Pearce pays, is, for me at least, a real and moving one.

Walter and Mary were encouraged by the reception at the private view, and after the Pearces returned to Market Place they received word from Madeleine Ponsonby of the New Art Centre that Bryan's work was increasing in popularity.

Bowness's introduction triggered a flurry of articles in several publications, such as *The Times, The Sunday Telegram, Arts Review, The Observer Review,* and *The Illustrated London News. The Times* reviewer noted with approval how "every detail slots into its place"; *The Observer* included a write-up in their Sunday "Briefing" section and illustrated the article with a photograph of Bryan's painting *St Uny Church, Lelant,* 1964; and *The Illustrated London News* published four photographs of Bryan's work with a double-page feature by Andrew Causey who wrote of the visual pleasure "when the eye completes its exhilarating trip around the harbour."

It gladdened Bryan that his parents were pleased, and after giving these tributes to his work a second cursory glance for the sake of politeness, he returned to his schedule. Walter and Mary could only smile and shake their heads; the thought of their son being self-supporting continued to astonish them.

Market Place seemed larger than their needs and lonelier after Margaretta's death and Audrey's departure. They also found the stairs to the studios cumbersome. A new housing development called Piazza Flats, overlooking Porthmeor Beach, was underway. The site had previously been a neighborhood of artists' studios and fish cellars. The new flats on the inland side were environmentally appealing with their granite stones and pillars, and a Barbara Hepworth sculpture stood at the entrance. The project was attracting many people, including artists and writers, who were ready to sell their drafty houses and cramped cottages and update their lives with modern conveniences.

With their declining years in mind, Walter and Mary selected a two-bedroomed arrangement on the ground floor. After the papers had been signed, they stood at the window and looked with some apprehension at the wild seas and punishing waves. Would they miss Market Place with its muted sounds of traffic below and the peaceful church opposite?

Bryan ignored his new surroundings—the approaching and retreating tides and clouds were meaningless to him. His townscapes remained cloudless and eternal sunshine still warmed his streets. Before leaving Market Place, he did paint a night scene of the Parish Church with its great stained-glass windows on fire.

"I think he finds comfort in everyday scenes of the harbor and streets," Mary told me. "And it is one way of expressing pride and pleasure for his birthplace. He does other things of course—he did a small picture of the chapel at night with a deep navy-blue sky—but he prefers to give his paintings sunshine."

H. S. Ede had followed Bryan's progress with much interest, and shortly after the New Art Centre exhibit he wrote Mary that he had found a gallery in Cambridge that would provide a suitable setting for her son's paintings. Arrangements were made and a one-man show was scheduled at the Bene't Gallery.

William Cooper, an art teacher, first visited the Pearces while they were living at Market Place. Cooper was to organize Bryan's 1995 retrospective exhibition at the Royal West of England Academy in Bristol. "In that attic studio, in 1966," the visitor recalled, "it was already obvious that the transition to profession was taking place." A painting on hard-board, not yet dry, and intended for an exhibit at the Bene't Gallery in Cambridge, overwhelmed the caller. He found it difficult to persuade Mary to sell him the picture but she finally succumbed to his entreaty and enthusiasm. The townscape had "an uninfluenced, commanding presence of its own. The subject was the harbour, worked in flat relief with the buildings on the lower edge of the canvas upside-down." And why not? Cooper speculated. "This was a view perceived by someone living in his own world apart from the rest: it did not require an explanation in logical terms. It was neither the painting of an adult, nor the work of a child, but it was clearly the work of an artist." Fantasy and reality were interwoven. "A precise vision eliminated that which was of no concern, followed its own rules and transcended perspective and realism. It prevailed over its own logic where buildings around a harbour do all face the sea and thus some may be regarded as upside-down or positioned sideways."

Walter and Mary took Bryan on a visit to the Cambridge area and realized that his urge to paint was more than just the need to record his St. Ives birthplace. The new surroundings didn't slow his production or intimidate him, and he brought to life with his individual style two local landmarks, the *King's College Chapel* and *The Round Church* with its three crosses. The two church views were acquired by Jim Ede for his Kettle Yard collection, and complemented the earlier paintings and drawings he had purchased when visiting the studio at Market Place.

"Round Church has just come into the house," Ede wrote Mary, expressing admiration for Bryan's progress. "I have a feeling that he has taken a great step forward arriving into that world of ineffable beauty which is so much part of his deepest nature."

"Bryan Pearce paints the essence of his experience," wrote Cecil Collins in his catalog introduction of the exhibition at the Bene't Gallery, Cambridge, in 1966, "and in the strange stillness of his paintings he is a visual poet, who gives back to us that exchanged world we all once had knowledge of, and we are renewed." In reviewing the exhibit, one critic noted that the paintings "cast pure sunlight and love across the room," and another hardened observer wrote with gratitude that "tired intellectualism was restored by his natural freshness."

"At this time in his life," declared Mary, "I could see there were no more traces of those violent and intense feelings he had earlier in life. Painting was a wonderful therapy, and he became totally absorbed in his work."

"Have critics ever suggested that he was influenced by the St. Ives primitive, Alfred Wallis?" I asked Mary.

"It has been said that he's been influenced by him," she replied. "But we had never seen an Alfred Wallis until long after Bryan had begun painting. Personally, I can't see any resemblance between the two."

"I suppose the French painter, Louis Vivin, has been mentioned because of his buildings—his way of drawing stone after stone."

"I know so little about these things, but I've heard the name. We've had lots of people say that his pictures are like Matisse's. A very nice couple came into the studio and looked at all of Bryan's work. The man said, 'You know, these could have been done by Matisse.' Bryan wasn't home at the time. I didn't say anything about him for they were complete strangers to me—I used to find it very difficult to talk about Bryan, particularly to people who knew nothing about him.

"When we went down to the lounge, he came home. I thought: Oh dear, here it comes! I introduced him to them and he shook hands very nicely. The man said: 'I see that you are very much influenced by Matisse.' And Bryan fortunately said 'yes.' I thought: Thank goodness for that. Then the man asked, 'Do you like Mattisse?' And he fortunately said 'yes' again. He had no idea who Matisse was. And with that Bryan walked out of the room. They wouldn't have known about him at all if I hadn't told them. He spoke to them in a manner which was quite correct. They were such a nice couple and so interested in his work that I felt they should know. I told them the whole tale, and they couldn't believe it. Bryan isn't influenced by anyone. He isn't because he's not interested in paintings by other artists, and he doesn't look at art books."

"In George T. Noszlopy's art booklet, *The Primitive Art of Bryan Pearce*, I came across an item which interested me," I told Mary. "Noszlopy pointed out that Bryan's signature will very often appear in the exact spot where he was standing when he painted the picture."

"I don't understand this," she admitted. "I always feel—when he is doing a harbor scene for example—that if he had another boat in the picture it would be one too many, and his signature just does the trick when another boat would be too much. Then in some paintings where he has a lot of patterns, and doesn't want his name to be very obvious, he puts it on some dark color where you can scarcely see it."

When Bryan is satisfied with his painting he will sign his name, slowly spelling out the letters to himself as they are placed. The two words "Bryan Pearce" are carefully written, and the location depends on his mood and the composition. They can be inscribed in the middle of a harbor scene to balance a trio of boats or on some granite block of a building to enhance texture.

"I once asked him why he had signed his painting in the middle of the blue sea," recalled Mary, "and he replied, 'Well you can't write on cobblestone.' "

Mary remembered him completing the painting of a church interior, and he hesitated before signing his name. She held her breath as he poised his brush over the "pure white altar cloth." She wondered if he would write his name on that sacred space, and if he did "how could I explain to him that it was not a suitable place for a signature?" Slowly and deliberately, he lowered his brush and spelled "Bryan Pearce" on the bare carpet in front of the altar rail.

There were critics who disapproved of Bryan's "naive compositions" and the "childish way" he signed his name. One detractor reiterated that the paintings imitated Alfred Wallis, and another faultfinder remarked: "I am surprised that one who is so alive to the delicate nature of rela-tionships can insert his signature with so little regard for its effect on the whole—the Japanese knew better."

"What do *you* think of Bryan's compositions?" I asked Mary.

"I know so little about art," she replied. "It's been difficult for me be-cause I can't discuss art with other people. My husband and I still can't really understand our son's work. We both prefer the traditional painting. In a sense, we're not much further advanced in our tastes than we were when he first started painting. But I do know, after having our son's pictures on the wall, I can look at other people's pictures and feel I no longer want them. I think Bryan's paintings can knock all the other paintings into a cocked hat."

"Does he have any particular method of gathering subject matter?" I asked Mary one day after having watched Bryan at work on a St. Ives harbor scene.

"He doesn't *paint* outdoors at all now," she replied. "But as soon as it is warm enough, he goes out and draws. During the early summer he gets as many subjects as he can before the visitors come to St. Ives. Then he will paint from his drawings during the winter."

"Are these completed on the spot?"

"Oh no. His drawings are so light I can't see the lines. I have to put on my glasses and struggle to see them. I never know what they are really like in the beginning."

"But he knows?"

"He does indeed! Once Bryan has his drawing the way he wants it, he goes over every single line was a firm pencil. Then you see the whole thing coming alive. When he's done this, Bryan goes over every line again, outlining it in yellow ochre if it's stone work, and green if there are trees. He outlines a still life in yellow or orange or any gay color he fancies. Everything must be outlined before he paints. And every stone is painted separately. Actually, he goes over his pictures three times."

"How long does it take him to complete a picture?"

"It depends on the painting. One with stone work takes four or five weeks. If he does fifteen landscapes in a year, he can usually get three or four still lifes done in between. He paints every stone of his little houses, one by one. And there are hundreds of these stones. When I see all these little houses, I say, 'Oh Bryan, look at those houses! How on earth are you going to paint them all?' And he will reply, 'I'll manage.' Then I think of what Bernard Leach once told me. He said, 'Work is not my enemy.' This is the way it is with Bryan."

Michael Tresillian in a 1967 article on "Cornish Artists" for *The Cornish Review* found parallels when viewing Bryan's disability and the afflictions of Jack Clemo—the "china clay country poet" who was blind and profoundly deaf. Clemo's mother, Evelyn, communicated with her son in their Goonamarris, Cornwall home by tracing words on the palm of his hand with her fingers, and she later taught Clemo's wife, Ruth, shortcuts to facilitate this tactility. "Fate has savaged them," observed Tresillian, "but, out of harrowing experience, art of considerable merit has been forged." Both mothers played a vital role, and both learned to type and to manage their sons' business correspondence. "Clemo toils in a long black night" and "Pearce paints in a naive, sunlit universe."

A darker side, however, was found in some of Bryan's early work. "In 1956," wrote Tresillian, "he painted a water colour, *Art School Interior*. The furniture visibly wobbles; the impression is of a picture painted in the middle of an earthquake. (It should be noted that Mary's explanation was that Bryan's hands were 'still very shaky.') In the same year he painted *Portrait of a Man*, one of the most frightening, nightmarish figures I have ever seen. Perhaps it was a nightmare. Or was it a doctor who examined him? His very first water colour, unfinished and entitled *Seaweed* (1952) also possesses autobiographical quality in that the struggling seaweed surely mirrored his own groping and mental uncertainty. Bryan Pearce, in terms of paint and individual character, has grown more placid, more purposeful."

Tresillian was immediately aware of the serenity when visiting the Pearces in their home at Market Place. There was "something deeper than the neatness, the order of the rooms. It is difficult to realise that tragedy has struck here."

The caller went to Bryan's studio where he got "the feeling of being suspended in mid-air, you begin to see *his* St. Ives, sloping granite streets, dominance of the church tower, boats and Mediterranean blue of the sea. The studio is orderly, no untidy clutter of paint or canvas, the serenity of the living room has climbed the stairs. Every painting is labelled."

Tresillian felt that Bryan's work begged the question Noszlopy raised in *The Primitive Art of Bryan Pearce*: "Is he the miracle painter of St. Ives or is he a representative artist of his age?" And there was the lingering question of influence tantalizing the reviewer: What about that other St. Ives primitive? "I can never remember seeing Alfred Wallis," Mary told the visitor, "and I only saw his work, for the first time, a few years ago."

Michael Tresillian left Market Place convinced that here was "a remarkable story, medically and artistically." He came away feeling that Bryan already stood among the elite of native painters. "Cynics may sneer, but I believe there *is* a miraculous quality about him. Medical treatment, the laying-on of hands, the love and devotion of his parents, the self-expression he has achieved in paint—all these have been factors in liberating a spirit."

Dr. Brian Kirman, a consultant psychiatrist specializing in genetic disorders at the Queen Mary's Children's Hospital in Sutton, was convinced that people of limited ability were underestimated and more emphasis should be placed on their potentials. He treated Bryan for a time and was familiar with his paintings. "Here is a person," Kirman noted, "with a natural talent set against a background of genetic hardship and he uses this talent in a natural unsophisticated and appealing way."

Professor Charles Thomas, in his preface to Janet Axten's *Bryan Pearce: The Artist and his Work*, observed: "Bryan Pearce...is a rare case of a major and natural artist whom Nature (or, as his mother Mary was convinced, Divine Providence) permitted to escape from the confines of a little-recognised disability that today can be checked and rectified at a very early stage. In itself, Bryan's delayed emergence into a new life and career was wonderful enough. More sobering, as one contemplates the volume, the quality and the impact of his work, is the thought that we might never have been able to see it. Any writing about Bryan must, from the outset, be in the nature of a celebration."

* * *

Mary came to our St. Ives cottage at Wesley Place for the second interview session in late December 1967, and during our talk she recounted an incident involving Dr. Woodard.

"Meeting him in 1958 was the beginning of our long friendship," said Mary, "and I can't forget the visit Bryan and I had with Dr. Woodard at his office in London last year. He said, 'Now Bryan, I want to tell you how good God has been to you and how many of my prayers on your behalf have been answered. Before I take your hand, I want to ask you if there is anything special you would like me to pray to God for?' My heart sank because whenever he is asked what he would like it's always been paints and records. Bryan looked straight at Dr. Woodard and said: 'Thank God for my painting. Thank God I'm getting better because I am improving.' Bryan has great tenacity of purpose. He will hang on and struggle against all odds. His one cry is: I must get on. It's never a case of I can't do it or I don't want to do it."

"Do you think he realizes that he is different from other people?"

"He knows all about himself," Mary told me, "and he's fully aware he can't do things that other people can do. My friend's son is a teacher. Naturally, Bryan always heard when David passed his exams. Bryan would ask me, 'When shall I pass my test? Shall I ever have a test?' Now he knows that David can't paint and he can. What other people have doesn't matter so much to him now because he's got his paintings. He once said to me, 'What a mercy it is that I have my painting. What would I do if I didn't paint?' And then he said, 'I would have my records on all the time, and I would get tired of them and be bored stiff. What would I do?' "

One of the questions I asked Mary was whether Bryan ever got lonely for people his own age. She had confided her concern about how he would manage after her death, and one day during a conversation with my wife, Mary admitted that she had been negotiating with a religious order that might be willing to furnish Bryan with a cell of his own where he could paint, and the proceeds of his work would go to the monastery looking after him. She was, of course, a mother placed in a difficult situation—there were no siblings or relatives in a position to provide a structured environment for her son—and she felt it necessary to make some sort of living arrangement for him since she and Walter "were getting older." When Stella mentioned that our daughter might be coming to visit us in St. Ives, Mary said, "Oh how I wish Bryan could marry some nice girl—I have thought about this so often!"

"I frequently worry about him," she told me, "and sometimes I'm terribly sad for Bryan because he does love young company. But of course one can understand that young people's lives are full and they wouldn't want to spare the time to be with him because of his inability to discuss everyday affairs. I do feel very sad when I see him always alone. I once said to him, 'I feel so sorry that I can't come to walk with you the way I did once. I'm not able to walk as you do, and you go so far these days.' He said, 'That's all right.' And I asked him, 'Don't you feel lonely, dear?' 'Not a bit,' he told me. 'But what do you think about when you go for your long walks?' And a lovely expression came over his face, and he replied, 'I think about my paintings and the next picture I'm going to paint and then I think about paying my bills.' "

"Does money confuse him?"

"Yes. He has no idea of the value of money, but he does know that he has to have money to pay his bills. He realizes that if he doesn't pay them he won't have painting supplies. Once I felt very ashamed of myself. He had brought in the post, and he said, 'Here's my bill from Lanhan's. Can I go and pay it?' I told him he didn't have to go pay the wretched thing immediately and didn't think anymore about it. In a little while he came back and asked me again. I told him there was plenty of time to do that. He looked at me and said, 'I have got enough money to pay my bills, haven't I?' I felt awful because he was so thrilled that he had enough to pay them and I had deflated him by my attitude. It was wrong of me. As soon as his bills come, he wants to pay them right away. He's so pleased to be able to do this."

Denis Mitchell and I stood talking before one of Bryan's paintings at a Penwith show, and we both agreed that perhaps this was the "prize" of the entire exhibit. During that evening, Stella watched Bryan go from one picture to the next in a calm and methodical manner, and she overheard one of the contributing artists say a little patronizingly, "Well Bryan, which of the paintings did you like best?" And Bryan, in a matter-of-fact way, replied, "The Bryan Pearce."

I told Mary what Stella overheard at the Penwith Gallery, and her son's reply didn't surprise her. "This was very funny," said Mary. "Four or five years ago I took him to Newlyn to one of the shows because he had some work on display. A few of the artists were kind enough to stop and speak to him, and I felt a bit annoyed with him because he only stayed for a moment and walked away. I thought the least he could do would be to stay long enough to answer their questions. So when we got home, I said in a rather peeved voice, 'Did you enjoy the show?' 'Yes, very much,' he said. I thought to myself: All right, my lad, I'll catch you out! So I asked, 'Which picture did you like best?' You see, he doesn't appear to be looking at them at all when he stands in front of them. And he replied, 'The picture I liked best was the one of *St. Michael's Mount.* It was mine.' He said it with such confidence, and yet with such humility. These two things don't really go together. But after you meet Bryan and get to know him, you realize that they can go together."

I probably upset Mary one evening when Stella and I were visiting the Pearces in 1968 at their Piazza apartment. My wife, Mary, and Walter were in the living room, and Bryan and I were talking in an adjoining room. He showed me a beautifully illustrated book on trains, and I described some of the steam engines I had seen before American railroad lines converted to diesels. There were two men in the cab of the train, I told him, the engineer and the fireman who shoveled coal to heat the boiler.

Bryan knew all that.

"And the steam blows the train whistle," he said.

"That's right," I replied.

"And without steam there would be no whistle."

"None whatsoever."

"And it's called a steam whistle."

"Yes Bryan," I said, beginning to feel uncomfortable.

"And the engineer blows the whistle."

"Yes."

"And the whistle..."

For the life of me, I couldn't at that moment think of some other function or movable part of an engine to divert him, and Bryan was in no hurry to give up his whistle.

Finally—and fully aware that Mary was in the next room listening—I remembered the engine's driveshaft. I quickly found a picture of one in the book and the subject was changed.

I did bring up this incident when I next interviewed Mary and we talked about it.

"Are there times," I ventured, "when his comments can lead to an embarrassing situation?"

"Embarrassing!" she replied. "That's to put it mildly. It can be dreadful! I haven't known what to do on some occasions. People were over yesterday to see his work, and I had said: 'This is our own collection.' Then when I left the room for a moment, leaving my husband and Bryan to entertain the visitors, I heard him say to his father: 'It's yours, it's Mommy's, and it's mine. That means it's our own collection.' He always responds better when I'm around. Just my presence will make a difference. I've never stood for any nonsense. He doesn't repeat things over and over when I'm there with him. Bryan knows I won't have it."

"I am overwhelmed by your generosity in sending our children's centre Bryan's beautiful picture—it is a thrilling gift," wrote one spokesperson when responding to Mary's unexpected contribution. Over the years, many hospitals, churches, schools, and charitable organizations have been recipients of Bryan's paintings and prints. This was Mary's way of reaching out and sharing her son's creativity. She also was generous to her many friends and even to admiring strangers.

I cannot forget that last evening at the Piazza apartment before we left St. Ives for Ireland. Near the end of our visit, Mary abruptly excused herself and returned with two of Bryan's oil paintings: one was a still life—I don't recall the blossom in the vase but the blue-red tablecloth is still before me—and the other oil was a townscape with Smeaton's Pier and several boats on the sand at low tide.

At first, I thought she merely was showing Stella and me the two paintings, but as we talked I realized that one of them was to be a going-away gift and we had to choose—in the end, and after much agonizing, we decided on the townscape.

"You've already given us two of Bryan's drawings," I reminded her.

"And you bought that little watercolor he did at Mr. Fuller's," she replied, obviously pleased.

Our departure from St. Ives marked the beginning of an exchange of letters until shortly before Mary's death in 1997. A transcript of our taped conversations had been sent to her in May 1968, and she expressed some feelings of uneasiness.

"I have read & re-read the interview," Mary wrote on June 20th, "and the words seem so different when written as compared with the spoken word. I think that the repetition of Bryan's name needs cutting out more

Bryan Pearce, 1968

than anything & just the few other bits & pieces which I have crossed through.

"On Sunday I packed our lunch & we went to Coverack which is just the other side of the Lizard Point & such a dear little place. Bryan took a board with him & he had drawn a wide view of the little harbour & the boats & he is now doing his second drawing before the outlining in his usual yellow ochre. (This drawing on board was for the 1968 painting *Coverack.*)

"Walter is wonderfully better, in fact quite himself again. I only wish he'd been like this when you were here—I did so want to take you all to a few of the nice spots around the coast, but we must hope to meet again one day."

"Today is lifeboat day & Walter, among others, has been selling flags," Mary wrote on August 15, 1968. "This morning at 9 o'clock Bryan & I took Paul & Sophie, ages 7 yrs & 5 yrs, Barbara Hepworth's grandchildren, for a short trip in the lifeboat as the crew were giving free trips all the morning. Unfortunately it rained all today until now 6:30 PM. Barbara H. is coming to see our flat at 5 PM tomorrow before going out to dinner with her daughter Sarah & son-in-law Alan Bowness. Their flat is next but one above us (for holidays only) & we often have their intercom dropped down over the balcony so that we can listen in for the children whilst they are out."

"Walter has just brought your letter out here on Smeaton's Pier where I am sitting on a stool with a rug around me for warmth," wrote Mary in a follow-up letter on September 1968, "whilst Bryan draws West Pier, the church & all the houses & shops along the promenade to the slipway. We came here at 9 AM as it was such a lovely early morning & I have stayed with him & have been writing letters.

"Since he has developed mentally over the years I find he gets distracted so much more easily than he used to do by people looking at his drawing & children stopping by & asking him questions. There is certainly no opportunity of going out anywhere here in fine weather without having many people around. He came home the other day feeling very distracted with his drawing of the harbour because children had been talking to him & he couldn't get on with it so I said 'Well, I should rub it all out & do it from memory' which he did & it has now gone off to the Open Painting Exhib of Northern Ireland & we hope it may be accepted.

"There is just one thing I have had in mind recently & I'm wondering if sufficient has been said about his general improvement in himself—how very, very much at peace he is & how wonderful he now is to live with—his thoughtfulness & kindliness & his willingness to help in any way possible, his ever present desire to please Walter & me. His pleasure at selling a picture & turning to us saying: 'Are you proud of me?'

"If you think any of these bits & pieces need to be put in the article please do so & if you think them unnecessary then that's all right.

"It must be lovely in Ireland now—how I'd love to see it & so many other places too, but then it is so beautiful here one doesn't need to go farther afield at our age though it would be so good for Bryan. It is the Holy Land that he always says he would like to see.

"We have booked for a week at Salcombe (a flat) in Devon, not far from Plymouth from Oct 1st - 8th. There are only 3,000 inhabitants & it's on an estuary & seemingly a dear little place & which may be suitable for Bryan to get some new drawings done. (*Corner of Salcombe,*

1968 was exhibited at Penwith Gallery, 1968; Bene't Gallery, 1969; Sheviock Gallery, 1969; New Art Centre, 1971; and Montpelier Studio, London, 1984. The painting now is in a private collection.) It is near Dartmoor & Plymouth so he may get an opportunity of drawing the interior of St Andrew's Church which, though being completely rebuilt, has lovely modern stained glass windows which may interest him."

"Did I tell you," wrote Mary in a November 21, 1968 letter, "that Bryan's painting, which had been sent to London to the agents for the N. Ireland exhibit in Belfast, was lost on the railway for 5 weeks & so missed a chance of even being looked at by the judges? Anyway, in the end we did get it returned after it had been found & we then took it to Plymouth City Art Gallery for the autumn show & it was reproduced in the W. M. News (*Western Morning News*) with a mention & now it hangs in our lounge. I will enclose a copy which you need not return & also a transparency of his latest painting which has been sent off today to Dr Denton who lectures at Manchester University & who since 9 years ago has bought five of Bryan's works. He & his wife are quite young & have two small children & now they say this has to be the last Pearce painting as they will have to start saving for the children's education. I think it's wonderful to know that young people are prepared to go without lots of things to enable them to buy one of Bryan's pictures."

"We hope you are all able to enjoy the nice weather which you simply must be having in Malta," Mary wrote me on January 6, 1969. "On Saturday it was like spring & the beach was used by young & old alike—it was lovely to see the children so happy at digging pits & making castles. Now today it is piercingly cold & dull & grey. Alan Bowness & family left for London this morning—I'm afraid they may run into snow showers on the way back.

"Bryan has 9 paintings on show at the library from today. Walter & I took them up this morning but I am terribly disappointed with the fluorescent lighting which has changed the colours completely & although I complained about this I'm afraid nothing will be done during the month to rectify it. Our flat looks colourless & drab without them, even though I've hung others up on the walls.

"An elderly lady from out of town rang up yesterday wanting to buy the *Church Memorial Jesus* painting which is in our own collection & today I met a lady who said she is trying to find enough money to buy his *Brixham* (1969) picture, but that & two others are booked for the Cambridge Gallery which only leaves three here. We have spoken to B. Tribe (Barbara Tribe, the sculptor who did a bronze bust of Bryan) over the phone & she spoke of visiting with you people in Malta."

"Yes, the small show of nine paintings at the public library has been a real success, I'd say," Mary reported to me in a January 23, 1969 letter. "So many local people who never set foot inside a gallery have been in & have been most enthusiastic, in spite of the lovely colours not being true because of the wretched lighting.

"I don't know if I told you this, but two years ago Westward TV came along & took a film of Bryan painting & of his pictures & when they read the script back to me it started off with this crippling mental disease etc. etc. & I told the director immediately that we were both of us sick to death of hearing it. He said it would make a wonderful story & I told him it was already known all over the country & it was about time Bryan's work was judged on its merit & that it wasn't fair to Bryan himself as he'd become a different person & so improved. So it was never put on & Walter said it was my fault, which of course it was.

"However, last Friday, after they'd seen the notice about the show at the library in the *Western Morning News*, the producer of the film rang up & said they were putting it on that evening & that only background music was being used & it was a good film. Well, it really was excellent. Everyone we've met in town has talked about it. Bryan was so natural & just going on with his painting as usual & absolutely relaxed— no one would ever believe a camera was so near to him. And so this has given him further publicity & after all I did the right thing by speaking up & then all that script was left out."

"It is early on Sunday morning & it is Margaretta's birthday today. She would have been 27 yrs of age," wrote Mary. "Last eve, I sat down to re-read the script & feel something more must be deleted. I hope it isn't too late & that you will be agreeable to it. It concerns Mr Fuller & if he were to read it, he may not like it & also another portion in which I've said Bryan's paintings knock out others if hung beside them—maybe this is not very tactful as I don't wish to get on the wrong side of our few artist friends, though I am quite truthful in saying that's what I feel."

"It gives Bryan such happiness to paint," Mary told me in one of our last interviews, "and now he so desires to know everything. He likes the best books; books that he can't read. An imbecile is happy doing next to nothing, but with Bryan there is so much which is right, except for that one little bit. Learning is his difficulty—reading takes time."

"Can he read the Bible?" I asked her.

"Oh no!" she replied. "The Bible would be too confusing and difficult for him. He can't even find his hymns when he goes to church. Numbers are hopeless to him. He doesn't know that 40 is more than 20, and he wouldn't know that 40 would be in the middle of the hymnbook. But he can find the hymns if he is given enough time. He'll start in the beginning of the book and work his way through, page by page, until he finds the right one. The hymn may be nearly over before he finds it, but once he has it he can read and sing every word."

As a way of encouragement, he was allowed to select his own books, and over the years his choices have been excellent. Lessons at home were set up, and often the visiting teacher assumed the dual role of tutor and friend. His assignments were structured to avoid the slightest complications—things that he could grasp on his own and remember—though the simplest task often appeared insurmountable.

"After our evening meal," said Mary, "he writes in his diary and struggles with his words. There was a time when he would spend as long as two hours every evening in the studio trying to get these words into his mind. Spelling them out aloud, like 'p-o-i-n-t, p-o-i-n-t.' Over and over."

"I have shared a small part in Bryan's week as teacher and friend for the past five years," Marion Whybrow remarked in her biographical account, *Bryan Pearce—A Private View*, "and have watched him gain confidence in understanding and discussing the context of his reading, as well as the mechanical ability to decode the written word."

These Friday afternoon meetings were informal, and Whybrow followed Mary's method of encouraging him to "think" while reading; an approach which appeared to induce conversation. Bryan carefully prepared his reading table for these five o'clock visits—his diary was open, there was a case of sharpened pencils, a book had been selected, and a set of dominoes was at hand to conclude the hour-long session. They began with the *St. Ives Times and Echo*. "Is there anything interesting in the paper?" he asked her. "I don't know, Bryan," Whybrow replied. "Let's see." Together, they scanned the publication, read aloud the items of interest, and discussed them. A photograph of the St. Ives Youth Band prompted him to say, "Could be a champion band." And then he concluded, "Ought to be in colour."

"His life is so very simple," observed Mary, "but he comes out with the most extraordinary things. The other day he said to me: 'Well, that's just a figure of speech.' If you asked him what a figure of speech meant, he wouldn't be able to tell you. Yet he said it in the right place."

A short word may be more difficult for Bryan than one of several syllables. Words such as *fall, fell, fill, full* can cause confusion and delay a reading lesson. Fantasy eludes him; after books on trains, Bryan's preferred topics are the histories of aircraft, automobiles and boats—such factual tomes may be on a reading level beyond his comprehension, though he does somehow assimilate information as he immerses himself in the pictures and illustrations.

Bryan can pronounce the word "medieval" but has no knowledge of its meaning, and when one least expects it he can use a new word accurately. One day when talking about old steam engines, he described a traction engine rally, and then stated that "they were in formation." One of Mary's friends, who was present during this conversation, remarked on the shiny brass band around the funnel of an engine. "No," Bryan corrected her, "it's a yellow band."

During a reading lesson, he came upon the words "deep in thought," and Mary, curious to get his reaction but doubting that he could grasp the significance of the concept, asked, "What do *you* think about when you are *deep in thought*?" And his reply was quite ordinary. "Oh, I'm thinking about what I would like to paint; thinking about my subject; thinking what I shall do next."

"When an opportunity arises," remembered Whybrow, "he will play one of his jokes on me. 'They lived in a little town...' he reads and then will pause and smile, 'called St Ives' he will continue. I am suitably surprised and we both laugh. 'That is just my bit of fun,' he will say, but many times he will tell me, 'You shouldn't make jokes when you are learning.' "

Once when he misread a word, he said to his tutor: "That's how you learn when you make a mistake....If you don't make mistakes you don't learn, see?"

"Quite right, Bryan," the teacher assured him.

Sometimes he will ask: "How did I try?"

"Oh very well, Bryan; you always work so hard."

"Yes, I do," he will answer honestly.

"Would you like a holiday from your reading?" This is a question Mary occasionally asks him, and his reply is always quick and definite. "No, I wouldn't!" Here is a person who finds sanctuary in daily routines, and he is visibly unhappy when schedules are changed.

His lesson was a pivotal point of the week, and whenever Bryan saw Marion Whybrow on one of his walks through town his first words were never "Hello" or "How are you?" but "See you Friday." Once in a more talkative mood, he went beyond this usual greeting and said: "Would be funny if we had Friday every day. What would happen then?...No Saturday, no Sunday, no church, no anything. Everybody would be upset." This sort of confusion amused him greatly.

Bryan's responses are direct: If the person in a story is "exhausted," he asks, "Is that physically or mentally?"; when Mary tells him that a doctor is coming to see his paintings, he wants to know, "Is he a doctor of medicine or a doctor of science?"; if a character in a story is depicted as "old," he will ask, "Has he got gray hair?"; and when a child is described as ten years old, he says, "You could say ten years young."

"Bryan's vocabulary is growing," Mary told me. "The bigger words he can sometimes rattle off. He can read a word like 'masquerade.' The other night he picked up Daphne du Maurier's *Vanishing Cornwall* and wanted to know what 'vanishing' meant. I had to explain the word very carefully. It would have broken his heart if he thought Cornwall was vanishing. He is this curious mixture of child and adult. Some of his answers can be so stupid, and at times, his answers are profound."

"We came up for the Private View of Bryan's 6th London show," wrote Mary shortly after the April 1973 opening at the New Art Centre. "It was on Wed 15th & it went off very well. We met many of our friends. Eight paintings are sold which is very good considering the present prices which have been increased considerably by Alan Bowness." The Pearces had gone up by train to stay with Mary's brother and his wife at Twickenham, and on their first day in the city an incident occurred which thoroughly challenged Bryan's ability to look after himself.

They were at the Piccadilly underground station during the 5:15 p.m. rush hour, and as the home-going commuters crushed forward to board the carriages, Bryan got separated from his parents. Before they could call out to him or get near enough to grab his arm, they saw a gaping entrance close behind their son, and moments later Walter and Mary were mesmerized by the blur of windows and a rear light disappearing down the track. "You can't imagine the shock & panic to us," recalled Mary. The thought of Bryan lost in the sprawling underground system was terrifying.

A porter, too busy to give the Pearces his full attention, sent them to the station master, and he in turn directed the distraught couple to the nearby Vine Street police station. As the minutes crept by, the situation became more intense; it was imperative that their son be found immediately.

A young policewoman recorded the details of the missing forty-four-year-old in a notebook, and when finding no physical characteristics that would distinguish him from the thousands of underground travelers, she turned to Mary and said: "Surely Mrs. Pearce, there *must* be something different about him—eyes? nose? ears? Isn't there *anything*!"

Mary looked at Walter and they both shook their heads. There was nothing extraordinary about him in looks, and the clothes he was wearing were casual: gray trousers, polo-necked sweater, and sport jacket.

"There is nothing special about him," Mary concluded, "except of course, that he *is* different! Most people find it difficult at first to realize that Bryan is mentally handicapped."

"Would he know where he was going?" the policewoman asked, and before answering Mary imagined her son being crowded on one of the seats of the noisy underground carriage, confused, and too petrified to call out for assistance. He had, of course, visited his uncle and aunt on numerous occasions, but Bryan would be unlikely to know where Twickenham was located in the greater London area. He had never written letters to the Warmingtons at their address, and the telephone was an enigma Bryan avoided. Walter sat clutching the red shopping bag his son had carried so proudly all that day until his father had taken it from him as they rode down the packed escalator to the Piccadilly Station platform. If only there had been some bright object, some parcel or unusual item of clothing to make identification easier.

"They got Scotland Yard to alert all transport, parks & stations," recalled Mary, but the process of "establishing a missing person" was slow and nerve-racking. The map of metropolitan London on the wall above them caused their concern to heighten—the odds against finding him in this vast area seemed insurmountable.

That April morning had held such promise for the Pearces. Another exhibit would further Bryan's career: there would be the long-awaited private showing and the opportunity of being together again with old friends. Whenever they arrived in London, one of the first pleasures was a call on Dr. Christopher Woodard—time spent with him was, for Walter and Mary, always a renewal of faith in their son's progress as an artist and an individual. It seemed months ago, not hours, they had left his office and were strolling happily through a park and along the banks of a pond alive with birds.

"It's always so good seeing Dr. Woodard," Mary had said, wondering what her son was thinking.

"I feel like a new person," he had replied, swinging the bright-red shopping bag.

More than an hour had passed since Bryan had been separated from them, and feeling that more should be done, Mary asked permission to telephone Dr. Woodard. She could tell by his voice that he was disturbed, though he was quick to reassure her. "Now you are not to worry, Mary," he began. "Bryan will be guided." They would be "meeting tomorrow, *all* of them," at the gallery, and she must not lose faith. If she wished, he would come to the police station immediately and be with them.

She and Walter would wait a little longer, Mary decided, before involving friends. Then the frantic mother responded in a way that had comforted her over the years: from her purse, she brought forth a number of postcard reproductions of Bryan's paintings and passed them around to the fascinated personnel of the Vine Street Station. "He knows and loves every stone in St. Ives," she told them.

Walter had telephoned Mary's nephew at work in London, and he in turn alerted his parents. The tense seconds continued, and finally after two and a half hours word came that Bryan had returned to Twickenham alone and unharmed.

"Where are your parents?" his relieved aunt asked.

"My parents are too slow," he replied. "They are still on Piccadilly Station."

"I was terribly curious to learn how he got to my brother's house," Mary wrote in her letter. "He had never been in *any* train before on his own so it was almost certainly another miracle & he had been guided home. He said he felt a bit of a shock but he didn't get excited."

Finding himself without his parents, Bryan had turned to the man next to him and asked: "Excuse me, can you tell me if there are many stations before Hammersmith?" "There are quite a few," replied the pre-occupied passenger, but for Bryan this vague return seemed helpful.

At Hammersmith Station, a lady was approached—"elderly like you," he told his mother. "Can you tell me where I stand for the Richmond train?" She showed him the location on the platform, and at Richmond Station he marched through the ticket barrier, saying to the startled collector, "My mother has my ticket."

A porter was next in the chain of inquiries. "Can you tell me how I get to my aunt's house?" Bryan asked. And the porter, not wanting to further complicate the day, suggested that he "get a bus or taxi."

A taxi was hailed and Bryan miraculously produced his aunt's address. In due time, the vehicle stopped at its destination, and on receiving a pound note from his passenger, the driver negotiated the fare plus a generous tip for himself.

After telling his parents everything, he asked with a look of concern, "Have I done something wrong?"

"No," they assured him. "You did very well, Bryan."

"His London show was a success," wrote Mary in a June 10, 1973 letter. "He will receive the same amount of cash for 12 paintings sold as he did last time for 18. Alan Bowness put the prices up a great deal & we didn't expect many to be sold really. In September Bryan is showing at Dartington Hall, & at the Beaford Art Centre of Devon in October. These are not selling exhibitions. Thank goodness. There were 40 American bowlers at our club yesterday for a game & tea. They enjoyed it as much as we did & apart from the poor weather."

Finding a suitable magazine that would accept both my interview material and photographs of Bryan's paintings proved difficult, but finally the work appeared in the autumn 1973 issue of the *Western Humanities Review* published by the University of Utah. Copies immediately were sent to Mary.

"It is a nice magazine," she replied. "Lovely paper & the coloured re-production & the other photos excellent. I suppose it is difficult for me to judge the article. I still feel my replies are rather abrupt perhaps & I would now (six years later) be more able & less scared to think of my words before answering. But Walter thinks it is good & in any case it is all just the truth. Walter is taking the mag along for the Vicar to see it."

I didn't have long to wait for the vicar's reaction and Mary's next letter.

"Since I wrote you I have loaned the magazine to three friends & to the Editor of the *St Ives Times & Echo* & also to the Vicar who thinks it is a marvellous article. Walter has just gone to fetch it back & no doubt he will hear more from him then.

"The others also think it is excellent so now I feel a little happier about my answers & I do of course realise that had I had more time to reply perhaps it wouldn't have been so spontaneous & the answers would have sounded calculated."

"I have shown your interview to quite a few over here," Mary wrote later. "But of course there are many friends & acquaintances who just do not believe Bryan's work can possibly be of worth & so I don't show it to them. Just as relatives & friends of poor Alfred Wallis—now they have had a plaque put up on the cottage where he used to live. It all seems so sad when the poor old man died in the workhouse.

"Bryan's latest church interior of *St Hilary Church* (1974) was sent off to Mrs Schaffer in Illinois (a collector) just three weeks ago. Some people think it is the best he's done though I personally think the one of St Ia (*St Ives Parish Church*, 1971) which you had reproduced in the magazine is the best. He is in the midst of painting *St Anta and All Saints* at Carbis Bay. It is quite a challenge as it is so very light & quite modern of course, all white & very light stonework & light oak woodwork everywhere, a real change from the darker wood in the older churches.

"Did I tell you Bryan now has one of the Arts Council studios? It is the one under Mr Fuller's school of painting. L. Fuller died some months ago. The entrance being in the passage where Hyman Segal's studio is. It is quite large but rather dark as the window doesn't face the seaside but on to Piazza courtyard. We chose this one because of the convenience to us. We can coo-ee to Bryan to take his coffee & it has given us more room in the flat."

She had remained in contact with Peter Lanyon's widow, Sheila, and in October 1974 Mary accepted the standing invitation they had for Bryan to sketch the house. This visit resulted in his painting of *Little Park Owles* which was shown at the Penwith Society of Arts winter exhibition in 1974 and at the Victor Waddington Gallery in 1978. The picture is now in a private collection.

"Your letter arrived just as we were setting out for Peter Lanyon's at

CBay for Bryan to draw the house," wrote Mary. "Just a short time before Peter died he said Bryan could come here to draw if he wished & so for these several years it has always been our intention. Now Bryan has just settled down to work & I am getting on with some of my reply letters & Walter has gone back home to do shopping & getting his lunch before going off to play in a bowls match with all the other Senior Citizens.

"Bryan & I will walk back later along the Hain Walk (the cliff path). It is really very beautiful here & absolute peace which is wonderful after the commotion in the town. There are thousands of people around & one has to fight one's way through Fore St. They are the wrong type of visitor to the town & all they want is fish & chips & all the boutique shops."

Bryan enjoyed having people in his studio to look at his paintings, but if Mary took visitors there when he was away, there was immediate concern upon his return.

"What have you done with the keys?" he would ask her. "Have you brought them back?"

"They are right here, Bryan."

"Show them to me," he would insist.

Training him to look after his possessions and to accept responsibilities had taken time. The lessons had to be ingrained through constant supervision and repetitive examples of what could go wrong if things were not managed properly.

"In every way, I am pleased that he reacts this way," said Mary, "even if I do find myself on the receiving end of my own teaching."

"One year when I conducted a tour of the studios," wrote Marion Whybrow, "I brought into Bryan's studio a party of fifteen visitors." He stood up as they entered and shook hands with each caller, including Whybrow who tutored and saw him frequently. " 'That's what I get for telling him he ought to take notice of people when they come in,' Mary whispered to me, but it was an explanation with a smile of approval. Bryan, always anxious to please, had responded in this manner."

It was "Open Studios" day in St. Ives and many of the people who stopped by to see Bryan's recent work were aware that he was preparing for a one-man show in London. A visitor who knew him and who had observed his rise in the art world with some astonishment, said as a pleasantry, "You're a famous artist now, Bryan." Instead of displaying false modesty or slight embarrassment, Bryan smiled with simple dignity and replied, "Yes, I am."

"I love saying to him," wrote Dr. Woodard: " 'Your latest painting is your greatest' just to hear him say: 'Is it really Christopher,' and he seems to glow and tremble all over; not with any arrogance or conceit, but a gloriously child-like and perfect divine expression of the beauty of all creation."

It was H. C. Gilbert of the Wills Lane Gallery in St. Ives who suggested that conté and pastel would adapt well to Bryan's drawing technique. Gilbert was right: Bryan knew how to use tinted paper to his advantage instinctively, and these hard and non-greasy sticks of color could be broken and the flat side used to shade large areas. The sepia range of color, from brownish gray to dark olive brown, and the shades of dark gray, black, and red-orange were perfect for his need to increase production—in both townscapes and still lifes.

His small conté drawings were done at home, and one day after looking at a vase of tiger lilies that his mother had placed on the windowsill in the lounge, he decided these would be a likely subject. Mary telephoned the local florist to order some fresh ones and sent Bryan on his way to fetch them. He returned home without the flowers, and she knew immediately that he was upset. "Where are the tiger lilies?" she asked. "They were in bud," he said crossly, "not the same as yours and I don't want them." A long conversation ensued as Mary did her best to explain that he had to be patient and wait for the flowers to open. Finally convinced that the tiger lilies were blameless, he set off once more to bring them home.

Bryan has learned to tell time, but it is difficult for him to understand its concept. He knows that an hour passes when he attends services in church and his reading lessons are of the same duration: "From five to six o'clock," he explains, "that's an hour." When his tutor told him, "See you later Bryan," he brought up this remark when they next met: "When you say, 'see you later,' it's later now—that's what you mean—later on is now." Perhaps more remarkable is his creative use of language as he elaborates on the time of day: "After midnight it is morning. When you hear the birds singing it is a sign of morning; shows morning is on the way. Here comes morning."

If someone mentions that they will be traveling to London on a train,

Bryan will insist on knowing the exact time of departure and arrival. "Is it the slow train or the one twenty-five?" he will ask. "When you get there, will you take a taxi or go on the underground or go by bus?" After these plans have been discussed fully and to his satisfaction, he will ask, "Where will you stay?"

"When I was a boy," he told Marion Whybrow, "I used to get over-excited when I was going on a train, but now I'm a man, I don't show it. I feel it inside. That's why you don't mind getting older because you understand more, see....Funny how things alter when you get older."

Bryan has had several tutors to help him read and write, and one of his teachers suggested that he keep a diary. "A very simple one," said Mary. "She thought it would be a good way for him to learn."

It proved to be an excellent method of improving his vocabulary, and over the years Bryan has taken pleasure in recording his daily activities. These entries, written slowly and neatly, with an occasional lapse in spelling or a forgotten word later placed above the line, are more than assignments. What he has noted belongs to him. It is there to establish his identity.

"I have been to church with mother."

"This morning I have been painting my still life picture in my studio."

"I had a long walk up the main street and down the Hain Walk."

"I have been to the library with my books."

"This afternoon I sat in the back courtyard with mother, with my books."

"I have been painting all day."

One would expect some show of emotion when there is an unpleasantness. The experience of finding himself alone in London's underground was rendered calmly:

"I have been to the city with my Father and Mother and then I came down from Piccadilly by myself because I had become separated from my parents."

In 1977, a painting of Bryan's was shown when the New Art Centre held its mixed exhibition of Cornish artists, "Cornwall 1945-1955," and Mary and her son traveled to London for a private view. The gallery had presented four one-man shows of his work. Bryan appeared relaxed as he looked at the paintings and politely exchanged greetings and mingled with friends and strangers.

Soon after their arrival Mary received a telephone call from Victor Waddington who asked to see her at his Cork Street gallery. Since she and Bryan were leaving London the next day on the midday train, Mary arranged an appointment on their way to Paddington Station.

Waddington immediately expressed great admiration for Bryan's work and told them that he would be honored to arrange a one-man show at his gallery. Such an invitation would have turned the heads of most artists as Victor Waddington was highly respected and his gallery widely acclaimed. Instead of being humbled and showing gratitude, Mary asked why he had not previously exhibited her son's paintings. Waddington explained that he was under the assumption that Bryan had made some exclusive arrangement with the New Art Centre. When Mary told him that Bryan was free to show wherever she considered suitable, they began planning the exhibit which was held in June 1978.

In the catalog introduction, Alan Bowness, then Deputy Director of the Courtauld Institute of Art, declared that there was "no need now to follow the evidence of the eye: things are as they should be, not necessarily as they are." There were preferred blues, greens, and browns as "touches of fantasy and imagination creep in." And Bowness concluded with: "Bryan Pearce has succeeded in offering us a new revelation of enduring insight and delight."

In an August 26th letter, Mary described this solo exhibition of her son's paintings mounted on the walls where the works of Pierre Bonnard and Henri Matisse had once been displayed.

"Bryan had an exhib. at one of London's leading galleries in Cork St—at Victor Waddington's, in June for 3½ weeks. The P.V. (Private View) was super—many friends as well as acquaintances & of course others whom we didn't know.

"Almost half of the paintings were sold & Victor W. has kept seven of them in his store which is a very good thing for Bryan. I will enclose this note with the catalogue which is well laid out but the colours are very poor indeed which you will, I am sure, realise." (She was right; the copier had needed more toner.)

Marina Vaisey, in a review of an earlier show—probably the Oxford Museum of Modern Art, 1975—had written in the *Sunday Times* that she found it difficult to determine why Bryan's paintings "have a distinct and moving visual presence, perhaps the quiet power of each painting has to do with a certain intensity, obsession and rightness, a consistency which characterises each fully painted piece of board....All Bryan Pearce's paintings provide their own refreshing and serene enchantments."

"I am sitting in the garden of Walter's old home whilst Bryan has a 'go' at drawing the house," Mary wrote us several months before her husband's death in 1980. "It is a lovely house & it used to be so peaceful but already I have a headache with the noise of cars chasing around two sides of the garden—it really is unbelievable." Walter had had X rays and the diagnosis was diverticulitis. "It has been a very hard time for me as he hasn't been himself *at all* but is beginning to get back somewhat to his usual self instead of living in a state of anxiety all the time."

Walter's funeral service was held at the Parish Church with a large attendance. He had been a familiar figure as he bowled with his "sports cronies" and chatted at the harbor front. Walter Pearce's good humor and benevolence singled him out, and he was remembered with affection by the townspeople.

Mary worried that the death of his father might interfere with Bryan's ability to paint. She grieved alone and didn't allow her emotions to affect his daily routine. This shielding gave Mary insights on ways to help her son cope with her own eventual demise.

There was a noticeable hesitancy in Bryan's work after his father's death, but the ingrained ethic of duty soon brought him back to his easel. What Bryan missed were the drives into the countryside—his father at the wheel and his mother nearby. Now the threesome had become a pair, and he had been told that his picture making would have to be restricted to St. Ives. There would be no more drawings of old churches and un-familiar harbors. The loss brought mother and son closer, and Bryan was more dependent on Mary. The little things she had done for him in the past were still taken for granted, but because of his inability to mourn and to compensate for the missing family member, he was for a time more demanding. She was there, as always, to sharpen his pencils, supply him with paints, arrange the framing, promote his paintings, and to make preparations for shows.

H. S. Ede, who had retired from Kettle Yard, wrote an appreciative and perceptive catalog introduction for Bryan's 1982 exhibition at the Falmouth Art Gallery near St. Ives.

If anyone is in need of peace, trust and joy, they will find it in the work of Bryan Pearce. He gives with his whole being, totally free of sophistication and totally altruistic; he paints as he breathes. These stones which form a pier, this blue which surrounds a ship, this island and lighthouse, this road, church, window, flowers in their pot, a thousand visual things, are the deep unconscious quality of his interior life and his immediate contact with his close friend God.

I know of no artist with whom I can compare him in this direct simplicity and devotion save Fra Angelico who would place one colour against another with assurance and tenderness, and yet, so it is said, when he painted the body of Jesus, he closed his eyes in humble knowledge of his own frailty.

Bryan Pearce has this inward vision, undisturbed by greed, desire of worldly achievement, concern with his own personality and much else; and such wholeness lives in his absorbed love, expressed he knows not how.

It isn't at all as a naïve painter he should be classed, nor even perhaps as a 'painter'—he really knows little of technique—but as an individual actively happy in reproducing the beauty of the visual world and his instinctive enrapment in it. I am grateful to him for this unhindered vision which is the deathless source of art.

Victor Waddington died shortly after Bryan's one-man exhibit at the Cork Street gallery, and the business was acquired by a partnership, Stoppenbach and Delestre. The new owners were pleased to continue the connection and made arrangements with Mary for a one-man show in the summer of 1982.

John Russell Taylor reviewed the exhibition in *The Times* and saw another emotion beneath the warmth of pigments: "There is sometimes sorrow in the sunlight which makes these strange paintings cut a little deeper....Pearce seems to be in direct communication with something most of us can only see in a glass darkly."

Whatever it was that Bryan had placed there could only be conjectured, and no conclusion beyond literary surmises would reveal the artist's intentions. After the handshakes and praise, the painter returned home unmoved and untouched.

"Are you glad to be back, Bryan?" Mary asked after one of his many exhibitions.

"Very much so."

"And what did you miss most while you were away?"

"I missed painting," he replied, "my walks through town, and cooking my breakfast egg."

Bryan has a daily routine at home with time set aside for outside activities: choir concerts, going to the St. Ives Arts Club where he is a member, and church events. He is comfortable with his schedule and often appears flustered when there is a change of plans or an interruption.

(He takes his membership in the Arts Club seriously—an organization established for creative professionals but now open to any person interested in the arts—and whenever his mother asked if she could come to a concert the club was sponsoring, he would look at her sternly and inquire, "Have you become a member?" After she explained that she wanted to attend the event as a guest, he would reply, "Certainly. You may come as *my* guest.")

Though Bryan's membership in the Penwith and Newlyn Societies had given him some contact with fellow artists, the St. Ives Arts Club has proved to be the ideal place where he can mingle with people who are sensitive to his limitations and willing to spend time with him. When a theatrical production is planned or a talk is scheduled, his curiosity peaks: "What is the play about?" he will ask. And before a speaker's arrival, he needs to be informed: "What is the talk about? Will there be slides? Will it be interesting?" When the club holds a dance, Bryan allows himself to be whirled about on the floor by fellow members. Unlike his sister, Margaretta, who could dance with spontaneity, he responds with broomstick rigidity.

He rises at 7:00, brews tea, cooks his morning meal, makes his bed, and is walking in town by 8:30. After this outing he begins work in his Porthmeor Studio and pauses for mid-morning coffee. He carefully locks the studio at noon and goes home for lunch. After a rest, he usually marches briskly around the harbor to Porthminster or Clodgy as he searches for scenes to draw. He returns to his painting or spends the afternoon in his room working on conté drawings. A tutor may arrive to help him read, and after dinner he writes in his diary and listens to music until bedtime. It would be unthinkable to work on Sundays, and there are the customary two appearances in church.

A major exhibition was mounted at the Tate Gallery in 1985, with international attention focused on contributions from West Cornwall artists.

Mary and Bryan Pearce, 1975

This "St Ives 1939-64—Twenty Five Years of Painting, Sculpture, and Pottery" event was proposed and introduced by architect David Lewis who had lived among the potters, poets and artists of the area shortly after World War II. These were the years when Naum Gabo, Barbara Hepworth, and Ben Nicholson shared their avant-garde theories with a younger generation of artists. Peter Lanyon, Bryan Wynter, Terry Frost, Patrick Heron, Wilhelmina Barnes-Graham, and sculptor Denis Mitchell, among others, had all felt impelled to turn away from traditional approaches. Bryan's work—encompassed in Victor Pasmore's definition that "a visual painter proceeds by a method of abstraction from the complex to the limited"—quickly was accepted by this group.

"Bryan belongs here," Denis Mitchell told me at the 1968 Penwith Society exhibit, "and I knew this before Mary asked if I would sponsor him."

Bryan's 1971 painting of the St. Ia Church interior and his 1961 oil of Portreath Harbour were exhibited at the Tate Gallery. For Mary, this

show was one of the high points in her son's career. As she made preparations for their journey to London, Mary realized that, with her eightieth
birthday approaching, she and Bryan soon would be unable to travel far
from St. Ives.

William Leah, the Vicar of the St. Ives Parish Church, was immensely
pleased when he learned that the painting of his church's interior would
be on display at the Tate. In a letter to the *St. Ives Parish Magazine*,
April 1985, he enthusiastically recorded his impressions:

I am actually writing this on the train from Paddington. I once
had a pastoral letter from Bishop Key written to us from Paddington
Station, so there is a godly precedent! I have been to the Tate Gallery
to see the retrospective exhibition *St Ives 1939-64*. It is subtitled
Twenty Five Years of Painting, Sculpture and Pottery. Almost the
last painting I looked at before I dragged myself away was Bryan
Pearce's *St Ia Church, St Ives, 1971*. It is familiar to all of us because
of the prints of it which he and Mrs Pearce have so generously given
us from time to time to sell for the restoration fund. I had never seen
the original before. It really is evocative of the spirituality of our
Church. Like all his paintings it is done with loving care, every stroke
of the brush precisely laid.

However good, reproductions can never give the true quality of the
original. It was a revelation to see the actual colours: the saints on
the roof are painted in gold for example, so is the banner to the left of
the altar; but I particularly like the balance of the large areas of the
muted browns of the woodwork, the purples of the floor and frontal,
and the off-whites of the walls contrasted with the brilliance of the
strong colours in the windows. And there was something I had not
noticed before: you look through the screen of the Lady Chapel and
your eye is led to the Resurrection Window. Yes, an Easter message
from the Tate Gallery! Bryan has painted it largely in reds. Red is
one of the traditional colours of Easter. Bryan Pearce's pictures have
something of the quality of icons: light comes through from the Other
Side. It really is remarkable. Visionary.

St. Ia rose majestically in the studio window at Market Place and this
edifice became the focal point in many of his paintings and drawings.
The earliest oil of the church's interior was completed in 1960, and the

1971 rendition was reproduced in color for the Tate Gallery exhibition catalog.

Several months after the Tate event, mother and son were invited by the Queen to attend the Royal Garden Party at Buckingham Palace. Mary told Bryan she thought it was "thrilling and marvellous" that they had been asked and explained to him how sorry she was that she must decline the invitation—Mary knew there would be much waiting and standing about and had found the journey to London for the Tate festivities "exhausting." Bryan was not at all disappointed, and he glanced at the crested invitation card without comment.

Every year my mother-in-law arranged with her bank to have a few pounds sent to Mary for Bryan's birthday, and in her thank-you notes Mary always wrote how the money had been spent. Typical was one dated January 5th (she rarely gave the year in her letters): "I bought a record for Bryan. It was one that he wanted for his collection, an assortment of pieces which includes 'The Russian Creed.' "

"Does he have an ear for music?" I had asked during our first interview.

"Oh yes, very much so!" replied Mary. "One day when we were going to church, we paused a moment before we opened the inside door, and he said to me: 'Mr. Jacobs is playing the organ today.' You couldn't see the organ from the door, but Bryan could tell immediately who was playing. This is how keen his ear is for music. If he knows a piece of music, he can tell you what it is on the first chord."

Marion Whybrow recalled a conversation she had with Bryan about a choir concert at his church. He told his tutor: "A choir needs an organ." When Whybrow asked why, he replied: "A piano is not as deep as an organ; it sounds a bit empty. A piano is all right for a solo singer, but a choir needs an organ because it has a deeper tone." "Did somebody tell you that?" "No," he replied. "I just know it." "What would you like to have been Bryan if you hadn't become a painter?" she asked. "I would like to have been a musician...if learning hadn't been so difficult."

He was delighted when the organist at his church gave him the opportunity to play the organ one evening before choir practice. The joy of allowing his fingers to roam the keyboard of this full-throated instrument was of short duration; Bryan's keen ear for the right notes doubled his disappointment. One can only wonder if his dream of playing the organ in The Albert Hall occurred to him as he began his brief recital.

For most of his adult life, Bryan has had a large collection of classical recordings in his room. Listening to Tchaikovsky, Chopin, and Mozart was preferable to time spent before television, though he did enjoy a telecast program called "Songs of Praise" and the radio broadcast "Listen To The Band." Hymns, particularly, are revered, and over the years he has studied his hymnbook thoroughly—he knows them all, though he can't locate them by page number.

There came a time when Mary felt that her son's musical activities could be enhanced by having him learn to play some simple instrument at home. She finally decided on a glockenspiel, and this was ideally suited for Bryan. The graduated metal bars tuned to the chromatic scale proved perfect for his excellent sense of timing and rhythm. This led to music sessions with fellow members at the St. Ives Arts Club, and one of his most memorable achievements—for Bryan—was his performance with the club in a pageant called "The Coming of St Ia" at the Parish Church.

He learns by ear the tunes he plays on his glockenspiel and is delighted when Christmas carols are included in a music workshop which he often attends. He has a special hymn, "Now the Day is Over," though his all-time favorite is "There is a Green Hill Far Away"—probably because of the setting. "I've always wanted to go to the Holy Land," he told Whybrow, "but mother's not equal to it now. If mother was younger I expect we'd go." Then after a slight pause, Bryan concluded: "Can't have pleasures all the time."

Every summer the St. Ives Youth Band gives a public concert, and Bryan is among the first observers to arrive—he enjoys watching the young people set up their music stands and listens carefully as they tune their instruments. It may well be that his reason for going early to these West Pier events is so he can claim a seat beside the drums.

Bryan's calm and pleasant demeanor impressed and surprised Marion Whybrow when she accompanied him to the St. Ives Infants' School for a presentation ceremony of one of his prints. He handed it to the teacher in charge, shook hands, and smiled when the entire school assembly applauded him. "Would you like to say anything to the children?" Whybrow whispered. "Yes," he replied. Bryan stood up and said, "I would like you to sing for me." He listened carefully while they sang *It's Love that Makes the World Go Round*, and when they were done, he said to

WHARF ROAD, 1955, Watercolor 12 x 18 ins., Collection: C. J. Stevens

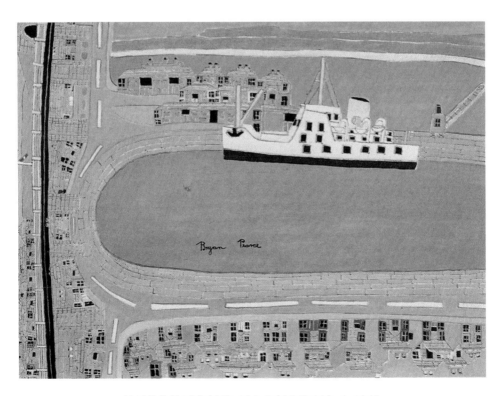

HAYLE HARBOUR ALL ROUND NO. 4, 1967
Oil on board 20 x 24 ins., Private Collection

ST IVES PARISH CHURCH, 1971, Oil on board 28 x 22 ins., Collection: Artist

THE CEMETERY ST IVES, 1975, Oil on board 21 x 48 ins., Collection: Tate Gallery

NORWAY SQUARE GARDEN (ST IVES SCHOOL OF PAINTING), 1982
Oil on board 20 x 24 ins., Collection: Artist

THE LADY CHAPEL, 1984
Oil on board 20 x 16 ins., Collection: Artist

THE MARKET HOUSE, ST IVES, 1985
Oil on board 24 x 20 ins., Collection: Artist

GODREVY LIGHTHOUSE, 1986, 24 x 34 ins., Collection: Artist

DAFFODILS ON THE WINDOWSILL, 1996
Oil on board 20 x 24 ins., Collection: Artist

ROSE'S TWO JUGS, 1998, Conté on Canson paper

ST IVES FROM THE TATE GALLERY RESTAURANT, 1999
Oil on board 24 x 40 ins., Collection: Artist

WHITE CYCLAMEN AND BLACK VASE by Mary Pearce
c 1960, Oil on board 21 x 26 ins.

them, "Thank you. I enjoyed that very much." Whybrow knew that Mary would be jubilant when hearing of this triumph.

Mary proudly wrote me that one of Bryan's new pleasures was treating friends to lunch at the Porthminster Hotel—a display of independence that would have been unthinkable during the early years of his slow and painful struggle. On these luncheon outings, Bryan made sure to get a table by the windows overlooking the railway station. "I don't know why steam trains excite people," he informed Marion Whybrow. "I expect they like to see the pistons and hear the train sound. Diesel trains don't excite you so much." And later he said, "Be funny if they called a steam train St. Ia."—the name of his church. "I would have a good laugh."

Jean Kennedy Smith, sister of President Kennedy, first learned of Bryan when she, her husband and daughter were visiting Cornwall. "In a gallery window," wrote Smith, "I saw a painting I immediately fell in love with." She bought the townscape of St. Ives and learned that it was painted by an artist with mental retardation.

Later, when arranging interviews for her book with George Plimpton, *Chronicles of Courage: Very Special Artists*, 1993, Smith wrote Mary asking if they could meet in London to discuss Bryan's inclusion in the project. Feeling that she was too frail for the journey, Mary declined this opportunity to promote her son's work. Instead, Smith came to St. Ives, recorded Bryan's story, and upon publication had a copy of the book sent to them. "For Mary and Bryan," Smith inscribed, "with admiration and appreciation for a lovely day spent in Cornwall."

"They invited me to their home in St. Ives—small and comfortable, with a large picture window that looked out on the harbor," wrote Smith. "Mary was eager to talk about her son. He spoke rather slowly. He told me he loves automobiles, trains, and how much he loved to paint. Afterward, we went to see his studio, a few doors down the street. It was very well appointed, with paints and easels scattered about, obviously the working place of a successful artist."

Bryan's success had meant a lot to his parents. "Before my husband died," Mary told Smith, "he went out for a walk with Bryan one day, and when he came back he said, 'Oh, well, things have changed nowadays.' I said, 'What do you mean?' He said, 'Well it used to be 'Hello, Walter, hello, Bryan'; now it's 'Hello, Bryan, hello, Walter.' "

It was no longer necessary to solicit galleries for potential shows: the interest in Bryan's work increased after the 1985 St. Ives exhibition at the Tate. Mary, who now found it difficult to keep up with the demand, was delighted when her son began drawing in conté and pastel. In fact, many of his admirers felt that these pictures were a "flowering" of his talent. In the 1989 one-man exhibit at the Beaux Arts, Bath, only one painting was returned unsold. (In recent years, Bryan has had some difficulty in controlling a shaky hand—it is no longer possible for him to execute the smooth application of oil paints that is found in earlier canvases, though some critics feel a freer hand movement has brought about an increase of texture. A slight uncertainty has been noted in the conté drawings but larger and more vibrant still lifes have compensated for this hesitancy.)

Bryan never expresses preferences: it is of little concern to him what he uses when the picture is underway—oils and conté are accessories under his control as he slowly and methodically goes about the business of filling his outlines with color. He may have a major oil in progress on his easel, and when he interrupts this work to complete pictures on a more modest scale with a different medium, he can return to the larger project as if he had never been away.

On an early morning walk along the cobbled main street of town, Mary stumbled and fell. She was taken to the hospital, and X rays revealed that her hipbone, already weakened by osteoporosis, was broken. Doctors recommended a hip joint replacement and surgery was performed. Several friends volunteered to look after Bryan, but this arrangement was of short duration. Mary, anxious to be home, wore thin her doctor's patience, and after twelve days of hospital care she returned to Piazza in a taxi.

Summer brought an influx of visitors to St. Ives, and among these many travelers were a number of concerned friends who called to inquire about Mary and Bryan. All this activity fueled her unhappiness at being confined to a chair by the window overlooking Porthmeor Beach. With the aid of two sticks she hobbled to Bryan's studio and later to the Penwith Gallery.

Then one day at the Penwith, when Mary got thinking about her son's contribution to the world of art and her long and lonely mission to preserve and promote his work, the idea of a retrospective exhibition began to shape itself. This was the site for just such a show: the early drawings at home, those watercolors completed at Mr. Fuller's art school, the first oils, those townscapes and still lifes bursting with color in the high studio at Market Place, and the recent conté studies that were becoming so popular. From the beginning, Mary had retained work from each stage of Bryan's development; with the future in mind, she had listed and carefully stored them all. Walter had questioned Mary's decision to keep these early efforts; he felt that they should have been sold and those that were inferior destroyed. Keeping some of the pale and uncertain water-colors and first oils proved invaluable for the organization of a retro-spective exhibition.

More than a hundred works by Bryan Pearce were shown at the Pen-with Gallery in October 1992. Some of these paintings had been loaned by collectors and friends, and others had come from Mary's walls. The long white gallery with its slate floor framed and complimented this varied collection. The early watercolors of interiors with their listing chairs and tilting tables aroused curiosity. The glowing colors of the Parish Church and a large jug on a patterned cloth highlighted the show. Along the main wall were the unpopulated townscapes with their calm harbors.

Mary, using her sticks, painfully made her way around the Penwith Gallery alone prior to the opening of Bryan's retrospective exhibition, and each painting revived memories. Their life together was all there before her: the hopeless years, the times of indecision, and the slow but steady rise to the radiance of recognition. For Mary, this was more than a retrospective exhibition of Bryan's work; in a moment of pride, she must have realized that it also was her triumph, a confirmation that she had done her best in giving her son a road to travel.

In the October 9, 1992 issue of *The St. Ives Times & Echo*, Frank Ruhrmund reviewed Bryan's retrospective exhibition at the Penwith Gallery. "One of the surprises sprung by their collective presence," wrote Ruhrmund, "is the recognition it affords of his ability as a colourist. A brilliant green still life study of a jug and fruit, skilfully spotlit at the far end of the gallery, says it all—it sums up, transmits and shares the joy the painter obviously finds in the physical handling of his pigment."

Ruhrmund noted Ian Mayes's description of "the miracle painter" and ventured that Bryan's survival as an artist was made possible by the self-sacrifice, support and strength supplied by his devoted parents.

A selection of watercolors and gouaches from the early period illustrated to the reviewer that while Bryan's style may have altered somewhat, there had been no significant change in his approach to painting. Here was an artist, "unaware of artifice, who would not know a gimmick, a short cut or a clever way out of a painting problem, if it were to rise up and bite him, he is a natural."

Ruhrmund declined to label Bryan as a primitive or naive painter and placed him "in a class of his own. A one-off if ever there was one, he has always broken the rules, quite unintentionally, and got away with it." What other painter would take such liberties? asked the reviewer—"for instance, would dare chop off the top of a church tower in a composition in order to concentrate upon its garden border, or use a bewildering variety of planes and perspective in surrounding St. Ives harbour with terraces of topsy-turvy, upside down houses, and somehow make it all work in harmony and seem quite acceptable."

The exhibition had been extended by popular demand, and such enthusiasm was not surprising, the reviewer added, for it "strikes a sympathetic chord in the subconscious of many of the viewers." It was Bryan's faith which fueled his work—"from the first faint pencil lines" to his "floating signature" which was seldom found in the traditional left- or right-hand corner.

"From his initial, exploratory, soft-edged watercolour still life studies of St. Ives," Ruhrmund concluded, "to a clutch of his early oil paintings: from an extensive collection of works from his middle years to his recent conte drawings, this is an exceptional exhibition. For Bryan Pearce is king, consistency and contentment rule, and long may it be so."

Michael Holloway, who would open the New Millennium Gallery in St. Ives, wrote Bryan after viewing the retrospective exhibition. "It was wonderful to see so many paintings assembled in one place. I think that all creative talent is a divine gift, and I feel that is especially true of your paintings. I visited the show on several occasions, and each time was conscious of the great aura of spiritual light and clarity in the room. I regularly visit art exhibitions, but I don't think I have ever been quite so moved and excited by a particular show. I saw you in the distance at the Private View. Shyness prevented me from coming up to you and shaking you by the hand. Yours is a real gift, communicating the spirit of St Ives and Cornwall following quite naturally from Alfred Wallis and the artists who have been before, but bringing with it something which is uniquely and unmistakably yours."

At this time, there was a remarkable development underway in St. Ives on the site of the old gasworks overlooking Porthmeor Beach. Sir Alan Bowness, during his years as Director of the Tate Gallery, had proposed a Tate Gallery St. Ives which had the backing of the Cornwall County Council. Some of the necessary finances were provided by the European Regional Development Fund, and many artists in the area, including Bryan, contributed works for public auction. Five picture galleries with space for ceramics and sculpture were planned, and the building was completed in June 1993.

Shortly before the opening, Mary was informed that her son's picture, *The Cemetery, St Ives, 1975,* was to be exhibited as part of the Tate Collection. For her this was a special tribute. "It is so exciting," she wrote, "& little did I think that such things would one day happen!"

Mary arrived by taxi with Bryan for the opening of the magnificent new building. The formalities were to include their being presented to Prince Charles, Duke of Cornwall. They were taken by elevator to the top floor where the reception was held.

Prince Charles laid his hand on Bryan's arm and asked in a friendly and informal way:

"Are you a Cornishman?"

Mary held her breath.

In a clear voice and with pride, Bryan replied:

"Yes I am."

Mary Pearce died in March of 1997—she was 91. Friends of the family wondered how Bryan would function after his mother's passing. Would he wander aimlessly without routine? Would the urge to paint diminish, leaving him rudderless? The one thing Mary relied on occurred predictably: the habits of a lifetime, so carefully and lovingly structured by her, gave him the necessary discipline without her presence.

During the last weeks of Mary's life, Valerie Dodds, who had helped in the Pearce household for more than a decade, came more frequently, and she was particularly attentive to Bryan's needs. The two had discussions on setting up his still lifes, the choice of cloths, and the flowers he preferred. She asked if he would like to draw the anemones which were in his mother's room. "Yes please," he replied. Dodds removed one of the flowers that had damaged leaves and brought him a number of cloths and several pots so he could make a selection. Later, when returning to check on his progress, she discovered that he had returned the damaged flower to the clump and had chosen an entirely different container for the painting. "It's my choice," he explained. "I changed my mind." Valerie Dodds had been impressed and Mary delighted. This show of certainty was an encouraging sign—a lifetime of discipline might well empower him to manage on his own.

A similar incident occurred when Lady Sarah Bowness presented Bryan with some hydrangeas for a conté drawing. "I'll think about it," he told her. The flowers were watered and kept waiting for several days while he made up his mind. Later, when asked again if he planned to use them, he replied with finality, "No thank you."

Bryan Pearce, October 1996 (Courtesy of Marion Whybrow)

Bryan was in his late sixties when his mother died, and he came through the trauma of his loss with a calm acceptance. He doubtlessly missed her terribly when performing domestic rituals—she was no longer there to be brought her morning cup of tea—but Mary had made provisions that his lifestyle would have every semblance of normalcy without her, and his career would be managed ably by others. The discipline his mother constructed for him is ingrained in the legacy of daily routine.

The cup of tea ritual is still in place—the recipients now are two guardians who have come to live in the Piazza flat since his mother's death. It is important to him that his working day has remained unchanged. After the morning egg and the making of the bed, he goes on his usual walk through town at 8:30 a.m. Upon returning, he opens his Porthmeor studio and begins work on whatever painting is in progress. He stops for mid-morning coffee—which he makes himself—and at 12:30 he carefully locks the door of the studio and returns home for lunch. After a brief rest, he works on conté drawings in his "bed-sit"—the room where he has his large collection of records and books on steam trains. There may be time for another walk through town before he attends some activity at the St. Ives Arts Club, and no evening is complete without the playing of records.

There was a supporting cast to act as Mary's replacement: the solicitor, Peter Dexter, took charge of Bryan's affairs; Paul Parkin was Bryan's accountant; Janet Axten, his secretary; Susan, Clare, and Robert were designated as Bryan's caregivers; and Sir Alan Bowness continued his role as art advisor and trustee.

A number of family friends are supportive: Del Castagli is with Bryan when he attends private views of his work, and retired teacher Win Cothey gives him his weekly reading lesson now that Marion Whybrow, his instructor of seven years, is involved in the writing of a new book. (This arrangement isn't to advance Bryan's reading-age level of eight years but to ensure that he doesn't lose contact with the written word.) His cousin, David Bennett—the organist who played at Mary's funeral—accompanies him to music recitals, and on Bryan's 68th birthday, Bennett's wife, Sheila, baked a birthday cake, and a gathering celebrated the event at The Mermaid in Fish Street.

William Cooper, in his "Bryan Pearce - A Reminiscence," concluded with these words:

To look back and reflect on those tentative early days at the time of the Woolworth's book, and the transition to the first water colours (which Walter Pearce was tempted to destroy) is to be moved afresh by the poignancy of this history. Undoubtedly there were sceptics and doubters, and jealousy too, as the talent developed and Bryan's works began to attract a serious following. However, the judgement of those who believed in him, together with those who advised, supported, and assisted, over a period of nearly fifty years, has been totally vindicated. Bryan now takes his place alongside Alfred Wallis, that other renowned primitive. They shared St Ives as a home, and probably neither would have flourished anywhere else, but that is all that they have in common. For every true primitive is an original, unique and solitary voice.

Bryan Pearce's legacy and reputation speak for themselves. Here, indeed, is a life which had to be lived forwards and to be understood backwards.

Among the many letters Mary received there is this commentary worthy of attention: "Bryan may be the painter, and his own personal achievement is miraculous, but neither he nor his work could exist without you."

"I have often wondered," wrote Dr. Woodard when contributing to Marion Whybrow's study on Bryan Pearce, "what would have become of his Mother's great talent for painting if she had not sacrificed it to her son's destiny, but then God always knows what is best."

"I'm sure it takes much of your time just making the arrangements for Bryan's exhibits and caring for his pictures." I said during our last interview, and Mary replied:

"As long as I have breath in my body I will do these things for Bryan. You have to forget yourself in doing for him. You can't lead any ordinary life. But which is more important to you? This is it. To lead a normal life or to do what you can for your children? It just depends on what a person feels. We didn't go out of Cornwall for fifteen years. Not a day! But in giving yourself you have given your child a life. To live without hope is such a ghastly thing. This is where I think the specialists are so wrong."

EXHIBITIONS

ONE-MAN EXHIBITIONS

1959	Newlyn Gallery, near Penzance
1961	Sail Loft Gallery, St. Ives
1962	St. Martin's Gallery, London
1964	St. Martin's Gallery, London
1964	"Exhibition 9," Fore Street Gallery, St. Ives (with Troika Pottery)
1966	Bene't Gallery, Cambridge
1966	Penwith Gallery, St. Ives (retrospective)
1966	New Art Centre, London
1968	New Art Centre, London
1969	Sheviock Gallery, near Torpoint, East Cornwall
1971	New Art Centre, London
1972	Sheviock Gallery, near Torpoint, East Cornwall
1973	New Art Centre, London
1973	The Cider Press, Dartington, Devon
1973	The Beaford Art Centre, North Devon
1975	Oxford Museum of Modern Art, Oxford
1977	Wills Lane Gallery, St. Ives
1977	The Green Room, Newlyn Orion Gallery, Newlyn, near Penzance
1978	Victor Waddington Gallery, Cork Street, London
1980	Wills Lane Gallery, St. Ives
1982	Wills Lane Gallery, St. Ives (two-man)
1982	Falmouth Art Gallery, Falmouth (early paintings)
1982	Stoppenbach & Delestre, Cork Street, London
1983	Wills Lane Gallery, St. Ives (two-man)
1984	Montpelier Studio, London
1984	Plymouth Arts Centre, Plymouth (retrospective)
1989	Beaux Arts, Bath
1992	Penwith Gallery, St. Ives (retrospective)
1993	Beaux Arts, Bath
1995	Royal West of England Academy, Bristol (retrospective)
1997	Beaux Arts, Bath
2000/1	Royal Cornwall Museum, Truro and tour to Penwith Gallery, St. Ives and Braintree District Museum and Art Gallery, Essex
2001	Newlyn Art Gallery, Newlyn, Penzance - shop

MIXED EXHIBITIONS

1958   "Arts Advancement Ltd," Sloane Street, London
1959   The Scottish Gallery, Edinburgh (with Guy Worsdell and
        Shearer Armstrong)
1961   Fore Street Gallery, St. Ives
1961   Rawinsky Gallery, London
1961/2 Taurus Artists, Chiltern Gallery, London
1962   IIIe Grand Prix International de peinture et de sculpture de
        Monte Carlo, Salon Bosio, Monte Carlo
1962   "Vergani-Sportorno 1962," VI° Premio di Pitturo, Incontro
        Gran Bretagna-Italia, Sportorno, Italy
1963   "Exhibition 7," Fore Street Gallery, St. Ives (with Giles Auty,
        Jeffrey Harris, and Tony O'Malley)
1963/4 Fourth John Moores Exhibition, Walker Art Gallery, Liver-
        pool (selected)
1963   Plymouth City Art Gallery
1964   Minotaur Gallery, Toronto
1964   Taurus Artists, Rose Lodge Studio, St. Ives
1965   Bradford City Art Gallery
1965   Plymouth City Art Gallery
1966   Open Painting Exhibition, Arts Council of Northern Ireland,
        Belfast
1967   "The Innocent Eye," Cambridge Arts and Leisure Association,
        Arts Council Gallery, Cambridge
1967   Municipal College, Bournemouth (loans from the Contempo-
        rary Arts Society)
1968   Travers Gallery, London
1968   Plymouth Society of Artists annual exhibition, Plymouth Art
        Gallery (selected)
1969   Bath Festival (St. Ives Group, 2nd Exhibition)
1969   Bene't Gallery, Cambridge
1969   Marjorie Parr Gallery, St. Ives
1969   Travers Gallery, London
1970   Bene't Gallery, Cambridge
1971   Austin Reed Gallery, London (St. Ives Group, 3rd Exhibition)
1971   "St Ives and its Artists," Magdalene Street Gallery, Cambridge
1973   Industrial Sponsors Exhibition of Modern Art, Congress
        House, London
1973   "Cornish Exhibition," New Ashgate Gallery, Farnham, Surrey
1973   First British International Drawing Biennale, Teeside, Mid-
        dlesborough
1975   Chichester National Art Exhibition, Chichester

1975   Second British International Drawing Biennale, Teeside, Middlesborough

1977   "British Primitive & Naïve Painting," Ikon Gallery, Birmingham

1977   "Cornwall 1945-1955," New Art Centre, London

1978   "Works on Paper—Herman, Hilton, Hitchens, Peake, Pearce, Yeats," Theo Waddington Gallery, London

1979   "Innocent Art," Otterton Mill Gallery, Budleigh Salterton, Devon

1979   Theo Waddington Gallery, Cork Street, London (with Terry Frost, Roger Hilton and Ben Nicholson)

1981   Wills Lane Gallery, St. Ives (with David Hazelwood and William Marshall)

1981   Bath Art Fair

1981   Beaux Arts, Bath

1982   Bath Art Fair (Stoppenbach & Delestre)

1983   Montpelier Studio, London

1983   "St Ives Artists 1983—The Penwith Society of Arts at the Winchester Gallery," Winchester

1983   "Prints from Cornwall," John Graham Fine Arts, Harlow

1984   John Graham Fine Arts Gallery, Harlow

1985   John Graham Fine Arts Gallery, Harlow

1985   "St Ives 1939-64—Twenty Five Years of Painting, Sculpture and Pottery," Tate Gallery, London

1986   "Inspire"—Exhibition of paintings, sculpture and pottery, The Royal Cornwall Museum, Truro, in conjunction with Three Spires Festival

1987   Pallant House, Chichester

1987   John Moores Liverpool Exhibition 15

1987/8 10 Venues, touring exhibition, East Anglia

1987/8 "Charles Causley—a tribute from the artists," Exeter University, touring to: Institute of Education, London; Southgate Gallery, Launceston; Royal Institution, Truro and overseas

1988   Trelissick Gallery, Cornwall

1988   "Aspects of Cornwall," Oxford Gallery, Oxford (with Daphne McClure, Robert Jones, Gill Watkiss)

1988   "The Cornish Collection," Artful Eye Gallery, Lamberville, New Jersey

1989   Beaux Arts, Bath

1989   Trelissick Gallery, Cornwall

1989   Mid Cornwall Galleries, Par, Cornwall

1989   "A Century of Art in Cornwall, 1889-1989," Cornwall County Council, Truro

1989   "St Ives 1920-1989," Beaux Arts, Bath
1989   "St Ives '89," New Street Gallery, Plymouth
1990   "Newlyn and St Ives Maritime Paintings," Falmouth Art
              Gallery
1992   White Lane Gallery, Plymouth
1992   "Artists from Cornwall," Royal West of England Academy,
              Bristol
1992   On-Line Gallery, Southampton
1993/6   Tate Gallery St. Ives
1994   On-Line Gallery, Southampton
1995   Penwith Society of Arts, Royal West of England Academy
1995   "Porthmeor Beach: A Century of Images," Tate Gallery St.
              Ives
1995   Gordon Hepworth Gallery, near Exeter
1997   "10th Anniversary Exhibition," White Lane Gallery, Plymouth
1999/0   "The History of Christianity in Cornwall," The Royal Corn-
              wall Museum, Truro
2000   "27 at St Ives Arts Club," St. Ives
2000   "The Innocent Eye," Mariners' Church, St. Ives
2000   "Twenty Years of Contemporary Art," Falmouth Art Gallery,
              Falmouth
2001   "27 at St Ives Arts Club," St. Ives
2001   "St Ives - eighty years of modernism," Julian Lax Gallery,
              London
2002   "Treasures of the See," Truro Cathedral 125th anniversary
              exhibition, Truro, Cornwall
2002   "Easter Show," New Street Gallery, Plymouth, Devon
2002   "Critic's Choice 2002," Newlyn Art Gallery, Newlyn,
              Penzance, Cornwall (selected by Mel Gooding)
2002   "27 at St Ives Arts Club," St. Ives
2002   "Still Life—a collection of modern British paintings, drawings
              and original prints," Julian Lax Gallery, London
2002   Market House Gallery, Marazion, Cornwall
2003   "The Print Show," Lemon Street Gallery, Truro, Cornwall
2003   "27 at St Ives Arts Club," St. Ives
2003   "Easter Exhibition," Lemon Street Gallery, Truro, Cornwall
2003   Anthony Hepworth Fine Art, Bath
2003   "St Ives September Show," Mariners' Gallery, St. Ives

INDEX